CHINA MARINE

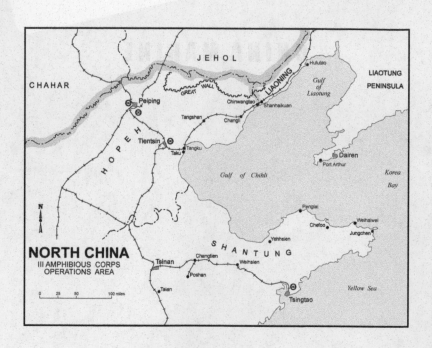

NORTH CHINA

III AMPHIBIOUS CORPS
OPERATIONS AREA

0   25   50   100 miles

CHAHAR

JEHOL

LIAONING

LIAOTUNG
PENINSULA

GREAT WALL

Peiping

Hulutao

Gulf
of
Liaotung

Chinwangtao
Shanhaikuan

Tangshan
Changli

HOPEH

Tientsin

Taku
Tangku

Dairen
Port Arthur

Korea
Bay

Gulf   of   Chihli

Penglai

Chefoo
Weihaiwei

Yehhsien
Jungchen

SHANTUNG

Tsinan
Changtien
Weihsien

Poshan

Taian

Tsingtao

Yellow Sea

Author of *With the Old Breed at Peleliu and Okinawa*

CHINA MARINE

An Infantryman's Life after World War II

E. B. SLEDGE

with a foreword by STEPHEN E. AMBROSE

OXFORD
UNIVERSITY PRESS

OXFORD
UNIVERSITY PRESS

Oxford   New York
Auckland   Bangkok   Buenos Aires
Cape Town   Chennai   Dar es Salaam   Delhi   Hong Kong   Istanbul
Karachi   Kolkata   Kuala Lumpur   Madrid   Melbourne   Mexico City   Mumbai
Nairobi   São Paulo   Singapore   Taipei   Tokyo   Toronto

Copyright © 2002 by Jeanne Sledge

First published by The University of Alabama Press, 2002
First issued as an Oxford University Press paperback, 2003

198 Madison Avenue, New York, New York 10016

www.oup.com

Oxford is a registered trademark of Oxford University Press

Library of Congress Cataloging-in-Publication Data
Sledge, E. B. (Eugene Bondurant), 1923–2001
China marine / E. B. Sledge ; foreword by Stephen E. Ambrose;
introduction by Joseph H. Alexander.
p. cm. Includes index.
ISBN-13 978-0-19-516776-4 (pbk.)
1. United States. Marine Corps—Biography. 2. Soldiers—United States—Biography.
3. World War, 1939–1945—Campaigns—Pacific Area. 4. United States. Marine Corps—History.
5. China—History—Civil War, 1945–1949. 6. China—Foreign relations—United States.
7. United States—Foreign relations—China. 8. Americans—China.
I. Title.
D811.S548 2002
940.54'1273—dc21   2001007378

The map of North China (frontispiece) is drawn from Benis M. Frank and Henry I. Shaw, Jr.,
Victory and Occupation. Vol. 5 of *History of U. S. Marine Corps Operations in World War II*.
Washington D.C.: Headquarters, U. S. Marine Corps, 1968.

An earlier version of "Incident at Lang Fang" was published as "Incident at Lang Fang"
by E. B. Sledge in *MHQ: The Quarterly Journal of Military History*, vol. 7, no. 4 (summer 1995).
Reprinted by permission of Primedia, Inc.

13 14
Printed in the United States of America

For Jeanne

and

For all the Marines of K Company, Third Battalion,
Fifth Regiment with whom I served overseas,
in war and peace, during 1944–46.

CONTENTS

FOREWORD

Some years ago I said to E. B. Sledge that his *With the Old Breed at Peleliu and Okinawa* was one of the best, if not the best, book on combat in the Pacific Theater during the Second World War that I had read. That judgment was not mine alone; virtually everyone who has read it says something similar. This is especially true of those of us who were not there but who write about the war and what it was like for combat infantry. So I asked Sledge, "When are you going to do another?"

"I only had one book in me," he replied.

But thankfully he had another in him, and he has now completed that sequel. *China Marine* is an outstanding work that will have a wide appeal to scholars and to general readers. We should all be delighted to have Sledge's observations, words, thoughts, and reflections on his wartime and occupation experiences. No one captures the scene, the setting, or the emotions better than he does. No one.

The war in the Pacific was much different for the combat infantrymen of the Marines than it was for those of the army in

Europe. In Europe it got cold—for example, the temperature was below zero degrees during the Battle of the Bulge. In the Pacific it was usually hot, and it never snowed. In Europe, when the Americans liberated a French or Belgian village or captured a German town, there was good liquor in the cellars—wine, brandy, more—that was either shared with or confiscated by the liberators. That never happened in the Pacific. When a squad of German troops ran out of ammunition and were surrounded, they came out of their positions with hands up. That never happened in the Pacific. The Japanese, almost to a man, would fight on despite having no water to drink, no food to eat, or no ammunition to fire. They would use their bayonets, their swords, even their teeth to kill Americans. And when all else failed, they committed suicide. The number of Japanese prisoners was astonishingly low, and most of those who were captured had been so badly wounded they could no longer resist.

Despite the differences, there was one striking similarity between combat in the two theaters. It was kill or be killed. Sledge is superb in his descriptions of what that did to men, to their feelings, their psyche, and their understanding of themselves and their buddies. Men who have been in combat together, he makes clear, develop closer friendships and bond together in ways that never happen in civilian life.

Sledge's account of his experiences in China immediately after the war is unique. No one has previously written anything of length about the Marines on occupation duty there. And his description of what coming back home to Mobile, Alabama, and civilian life were like for him are vivid, lively, personally touching, and most of all contain his keen observations and sense of his own being. The passages about his father made me weep.

China Marine will have legs to it. The book will last. Like *With the Old Breed*, it will be read, appreciated, and taught, now and for decades to come. We, all of us, will be indebted to E. B. Sledge for having written it and will thank God that, as it turned out, he did have one more book in him.

Stephen E. Ambrose
New Orleans, 2001

PREFACE

Like most other surviving veterans of World War II, the war remains the most significant experience in my life—not the best experience, nor the most fulfilling, but unequivocally the most significant.

I was young and naive, away from home and my country for the first time. The war for me, a Marine infantryman, was many things—overwhelming, horrifying, degrading, fascinating. I somehow survived two of the most prolonged and lethal battles of the war, Peleliu and Okinawa, when so many good, promising young men did not and so many more came home without their limbs, or their eyes, or their minds.

Yet I wouldn't say I was untouched by close combat. I would be haunted by vivid, terrifying nightmares for the next twenty years or so. And I was particularly morose and fatalistic after the second battle. Just about every one of my buddies in K Company, Third Battalion, Fifth Marines (K/3/5) had been killed or mangled. And while a good number would return to our ranks from field hospitals, we all knew that Gen. Douglas MacArthur was already planning our role in the next damned landing, the biggest one in history, Operation CORONET, right down the gut to Tokyo. None of us combat veterans expected to survive that epic carnage.

The A-bombs saved my life, saved my buddies' lives, and most decidedly saved the lives of millions of Japanese, civilian as well as military.

On a personal level, my experiences in North China on occupation duty with the First Marine Division began the slow healing process—especially the felicitous experience of being befriended by the family of Dr. Y. K. Soong and the remarkable Flemish priest Fr. Marcel von Hemelryjck. They were my personal bridge back to civilization and culture after so many months of killing. In this way I began cleansing myself, layer by psychological layer, of the accumulated horrors I had witnessed and performed as a Marine infantryman at Peleliu and Okinawa. It wasn't the whole cure by any means, but dear Lord, it was the essential beginning.

Other amenities of peace helped me overcome this embedded trauma (for that's what I brought home from the war, the emotional equivalent of a sliver of steel shrapnel lodged near my heart). Foremost of these amenities was the abiding love of my wife, Jeanne. Twenty years ago she encouraged me to write *With the Old Breed at Peleliu and Okinawa*. Now she has inspired me to write this sequel.

So this small book has two objectives. First, I wanted to share my impressions of being a twenty-three-year-old youngster from southern Alabama trying to shake off the shadows of close combat and then experiencing dangerous duty and exotic liberty in one of the oldest and most cosmopolitan cities in the world. I also wanted to describe my troubled homecoming and difficult adjustment to a virtually oblivious America as well as my cumulative and rather jaundiced views on the real costs of war. As recorded in *With the Old Breed*, I experienced some unspeakable things in close combat. I refuse to abide anyone now who seeks to either glorify or trivialize those realities.

I want to express my gratitude for the help of and the suggestions from Col. Joseph H. Alexander, USMC (ret.). This book would not have been possible without Joe's friendship, ideas, editing, suggestions, and contributions. I cannot thank him enough for his good-natured help—and wonderful sense of humor. I'm also appreciative of the assistance and encouragement of Mr. Lou Reda of Easton, Pennsylvania, whose production company created the excellent TV documentaries on Peleliu and Okinawa for The History Channel in 1995. And I especially want to thank my wife, Jeanne, for her love and many suggestions—and her patience in living happily with someone whose mind often dwells in the past.

Special thanks go to my son, John, for bringing the manuscript to the attention of The University of Alabama Press, and to my daughter-in-law, Lynn, for her assistance in shaping it for publication.

Thanks also to two longsuffering typists who transformed my scrawls of yesteryear into legible form, Melene Tuton Patchel and Judy Akin, and also to The University of Alabama Press for making this book a reality.

The bulk of this book is new material, derived principally from my notes maintained at the time in Okinawa, North China, and during the long transit home. Together, these accounts reflect what I experienced during the end of the Pacific War and the occupation of North China, my homecoming, and my difficult passage to peace.

Eugene B. Sledge
Montevallo, Alabama
1999

INTRODUCTION

Thousands of readers came to know Eugene B. Sledge, a World War II Marine veteran and retired biology professor, through his landmark book *With the Old Breed at Peleliu and Okinawa*, which historians have acclaimed as the definitive enlisted man's memoir of World War II.

Peleliu remains the bitterest fight the U.S. Marine Corps ever experienced, a heartless meat grinder that came close to wrecking its oldest division. Okinawa proved to be a more meaningful battle, but the fighting was rife with horrors and consumed the farms, villages, and graveyards of a gentle people who would lose one-third of their population in the maelstrom. Young Private First Class Sledge (age twenty at Peleliu) survived both those murderous battles despite sustained exposure in the front lines as an infantryman serving in a rifle company of the First Marine Division, nicknamed the "Old Breed." A photograph taken of Sledge at the end of Okinawa reflects a young man with the classic "thousand-yard stare" of combat fatigue. His subsequent memoir, graphic and horrifying, transported the reader to the very gates of hell. His book would strike a special chord with veteran infantrymen of any service or theater of combat. "Thanks for telling *my* story," many would later write.

At the height of the Pacific War, tired of waiting for his academic degree and officer's commission, Sledge left Georgia Tech and enlisted in the Marines. He was a doctor's son, well-raised and widely read. He could have qualified for many technical, rear-echelon assignments. Instead he volunteered for the infantry. He joined the Old Breed at their advance base in the Russell Islands just in time for the bloody assault on Peleliu on 15 September 1944.

The First Marine Division sustained 6,500 casualties at Peleliu and 7,500 more at Okinawa the following spring. Sledge's rifle company suffered proportionate losses. Of the 240 men who landed at D-Day on Peleliu, all but Sledge and nine others were killed or wounded by the end of the Okinawa campaign. Yet his physical survival came at the price of a staggering emotional burden. "None came out unscathed," he would write.

Forbidden to maintain a diary in combat, Sledge resorted to recording his traumatic observations in the margins of the New Testament he carried. Years later, these extracted remarks became the basis for *With the Old Breed.* His original editors chose to terminate his account shortly after the surrender of Japan. It was the logical stopping point, although decidedly not the *psychological* stopping point. Both Sledge and many of his readers felt the abrupt ending was too much like an amputation, that more of the story remained to be told.

Sledge's memorable experiences did not end with the cessation of hostilities at Okinawa. For him and his comrades in arms, there awaited the mission of disarming the immense and undefeated Japanese armies on the Asian mainland, the establishment of order out of chaos, and the initial keeping of the peace so painstakingly secured. Then, for infantrymen so long engaged in the savage and surreal world of close combat, there remained the personal mission of coming home, seeking normalcy, and dealing with their suppressed memories, fears, and guilt. Sledge's first book, indelible as it was, did not provide the emotional closure that for so long eluded him and evidently many other readers.

This book provides that closure.

Here Sledge describes his often intriguing and sometimes dangerous experiences on occupation duty in North China in the epicenter of the competing forces that convulsed that troubled nation. He describes his delayed and uneasy homecoming to a changed America and frankly admits his difficulties and false starts in attempting to adapt to a life without war. He conveys the crippling effects of the violent nightmares that haunted him long after the guns grew silent.

For Eugene Sledge, the long healing process actually began during his postwar occupation duty in China, an episodic but largely forgotten chapter of Marine Corps history.

The First Marine Division drew the mission of redeploying from Okinawa to North China as the lead combat element of the Third Amphibious Corps, commanded by Iwo Jima veteran Maj. Gen. Keller E. Rockey.

North China in the late summer of 1945 was a tinderbox of conflicting armed forces scraping against each other like giant tectonic plates. Few nations suffered more tragically in World War II than did China. But its seven-year war with Japan barely ended before the starving, dispossessed people experienced an eruption of the long-simmering civil war between the reactionary forces of Generalissimo Chiang Kai-shek and the revolutionary Communists of Mao Tse-tung. Other heavily armed bands stalked the region, some former puppet troops trained by the Japanese, others opportunistic brigands led by warlords. There was also the possibility of an attempted Soviet extension into China proper from their newly acquired territory in Manchuria. Large parts of North China were literally up for grabs. The Marines, who had figured their most dangerous job would be disarming and repatriating the two-thirds of a million Japanese soldiers in Hopeh Province, would come to regard the compliant, disciplined Japanese as their most reliable ally in these treacherous times.

The First Marine Division would spend two years in North China, from its initial landing at Taku on 30 September 1945 until the withdrawal of its rear echelon on 1 September 1947. Their main antagonists proved to be the Chinese Communists, especially when American pilots began transporting large numbers of Chiang Kai-shek's forces into the province. Dangerous confrontations occurred frequently. Firefights erupted that led to American and Chinese casualties. It was a harbinger. Five years later the First Marine Division would be battling for its very survival against eight Chinese Communist divisions around North Korea's Chosin Reservoir in one of the greatest fighting withdrawals in military history.

If Mao's Eighth Route Army viewed the Old Breed as just one more foreign invader to be forced out of China, the people of Hopeh Province looked at the Marines as their saviors. When the Old Breed landed from their troop ships anchored in the Gulf of Chihli and proceeded up the familiar road to Tientsin and Peiping—the route their forebears fought to traverse during the Boxer Rebellion in 1900—they encountered tens of thousands of natives genuinely excited by their triumphant entry. The whole event was a marvelous tonic for these Marines, whose campaigns had been waged in battlegrounds largely devoid of civilian populations. One veteran described the experience as "a victory parade . . . that must have outshone, outshouted, and outsmelled any welcome given to troops any time, any place, and anywhere during the war."

Most Marine infantrymen served their time in North China guarding the trains, bridges, and depots that kept the huge cities of Tientsin and Peiping supplied with food and coal for the winter. The supply trains proved an attractive target for the other armed forces roaming the land, and in just the first month after their arrival, Marines engaged in firefights along the railroad right-of-ways on three occasions.

PFC Sledge's regiment, the Fifth Marines, had the good fortune of being headquartered in Peiping, the ancient capital of the Chinese Empire (it was *Peking* for five hundred years until the seat of government moved to Nanking in 1928, then *Peiping* until 1949, when overrun by the Chinese Communists). Strategically sited thirty-five miles south of the Great Wall and seventy miles northwest of Tientsin, Peiping in 1945 was both a critical rail junction and the cultural and intellectual center of the stricken nation. Fittingly, the Fifth Marines established their headquarters near the old U.S. Marine Corps barracks in the Legation Quarter of the Inner, or Tatar, City, just to the northeast of the towering Chien Men Gate.

For PFC Sledge, young and a very long way from his home in Mobile, Alabama, the abrupt immersion into this swarming, exotic city proved a galvanic experience. He was surrounded by millions of Chinese, a totally foreign but fascinating society. The young man made friends, picked up the language, and learned Chinese history and culture. In time, the Soong family befriended him.

Sledge had been raised in a close-knit family that combined a love for outdoor life with an appreciation for classical music and spirited discourse. The Soong family provided a similar environment, and Sledge spent many off-duty hours enjoying their hospitality. These visits provided two great benefits for the homesick, war-scarred Marine—a civilized alternative to the typical binge-and-boredom cycle of his contemporaries, and a gradual decompression from some of the most vivid memories of Peleliu's Bloody Nose Ridge or Okinawa's Half Moon Hill. Quite likely, the kindness of the Soongs preserved Sledge's sanity.

This felicitous interlude would not last. Sledge's rotation number came up in February 1946, and he bid farewell to the Soongs to begin his long journey home to America. The Soongs' days were numbered. Less than two years later, the Chinese Communists captured Peiping, and the family disappeared.

The young veteran returned to Mobile proud of his service with the Old Breed, scornful of those who never served in harm's way, but increasingly aware of how things had changed in his absence. The war had changed him too. He could no longer kill deer or doves with his erstwhile hunting pals, for example. But neither could he fit in with the society he had left two years earlier. Despite rampant peace and prosperity—and the munificence of the G.I. Bill—he spun his wheels searching for his place and a profession. "Didn't the Marines teach you *anything?*" demanded a frustrated registrar at Auburn. "Yes, Ma'am," Sledge replied icily. "They taught me how to kill Japs." For this acquired skill, however, there could be no academic credit.

Sledge dutifully attained a business degree, then for awhile sold insurance and real estate, but his heart lay elsewhere, and his memories continued to haunt him. His father, who had treated World War I victims of combat fatigue, advised him to reject self-pity and find his own relative peace. "Get an outdoor job, enjoy good books and good music, study the diversity of life," he told his son. Sledge's new wife, Jeanne, quietly helped him deal with his flashbacks and find meaningful work.

Returning to Auburn for a graduate degree in plant pathology, Sledge at first intended to operate his own flower nursery, but his research opened many other doors. Entranced by the overall study of nature, he then pursued his Ph.D. degree in biology and biochemistry at the University of Florida, describing with relish his years of graduate work as "an intellectual boot camp." He would later admit that his lifelong study of nature had served to keep his memories from driving him insane. "He loved the out-of-doors," his wife Jeanne recalled, "and he didn't just walk, he paid close attention to every bird, every leaf, every bug that he encountered. He drew so much strength from nature."

For the next twenty-eight years, Dr. Sledge taught biology to undergraduate students at the University of Montevallo, located in an attractive small town thirty miles south of Birmingham, Alabama. He and Jeanne built a home on a two-acre wooded lot and named the place "Stillwood." Here they raised their two sons and delighted in the frequent company of his students.

President emeritus and former music professor John W. Stewart spoke fondly of the years he and Eugene Sledge were neighbors and associates at the university. "Gene had a deep interest in classical music," he said, "and this proved very useful to finding within that music and so within himself a sense of order and propriety and beauty which helped him exorcise some of his demons."

Sledge's students found him to be both a stern disciplinarian and yet a man with a legendary humor. Prof. Malcolm R. Braid, one of several students in "Uncle Eugene's" class who came back to Montevallo to teach biology alongside Sledge, provided a sample of his mentor's humor: "Dr. Sledge!" one student exclaimed during the obligatory bird walk, "Look at that *enormous* bird! What is it?" Sledge raised his binoculars and gasped. There in the nearest tree perched an unmistakable cormorant, a seabird—yet the Gulf of Mexico lay two hundred miles away. Sledge sputtered until he noticed his students rolling on the ground in mirth. They had purloined a stuffed bird from the museum and tied it to the tree. "No one laughed louder than Uncle Eugene," Braid recalled, adding, "He always made learning fun."

Under these benevolent conditions, Sledge's nightmares finally began to subside. It helped, he discovered, to write down the particularly painful memories, and he began to do this, extracting his original notes from the margins of his dog-eared Bible. In time, these individual anecdotes began to coalesce into natural sections and chapters. Jeanne encouraged him to write out the whole story, if only to get the nightmares fully exposed. Sledge then undertook the mission of telling the entire range of his experiences at Peleliu and Okinawa for his family—and also for his buddies in K Company, living and dead. He wrote a thousand pages by hand. By the late 1970s, he had assembled the manuscript for *With the Old Breed.* The published book's subsequent success never affected Sledge's perspective. "All I tried to do was tell people how bad things were in those days," he said.

The final chapter of that volume is entitled "The End of the Agony." In view of his decades of flashback nightmares, we may well ask ourselves, "Does the agony ever end?" Sledge's bad memories were assuaged by his love of nature, teaching, and good music; by the loving support of his wife and sons; and—initially—by his wholesome experiences in the cosmopolitan city of Peiping in 1945 and 1946.

Dr. Eugene B. Sledge died at Stillwood on 3 March 2001 at the age of seventy-seven. He was buried with military honors in Mobile. His first book remains in print, two decades after its publication.

Semper Fidelis, Sledgehammer!

Joseph H. Alexander
Colonel, USMC (Ret.)

CHINA MARINE

In the fall of 1945, there existed in China a power vacuum that many opposing factions stood ready to fill. Into this seething cauldron of political and ideological unrest we arrived—the survivors of the battle for Okinawa—more like schoolboys on holiday than mighty conquerors. As veterans of the First Marine Division, we had already satisfied our quest for adventure. We wanted only peace and quiet and a chance to experience life without bloodshed—life where there was a reasonable hope of a future. In North China in 1945–46, however, we found peace and quiet to be elusive qualities. We also discovered in ancient Peiping an exotic, urbane society living out its last days in the face of dangerous and overwhelming changes.

TENT CAMP, NORTHERN OKINAWA, AFTER THE BATTLE

Our eighty-two-day battle was over, but the endless war continued. We scrubbed the accumulated filth off our bodies, cleaned our weapons and other combat gear, and began the long process of preparing for the next invasion, God forbid. None of us survivors expected our luck to continue.

Large fleets of aircraft, mostly B-29 bombers and their fighter escorts, passed high over our camp every day on their way to bomb Japan. The number of planes in these raids was incredible. We would hear a low rumbling drone of motors, and everyone would run out of their tents and start craning their necks as we all looked up at the sky. The flights of planes sometimes stretched as far as we could see, and the air reverberated with the sound of their throbbing engines.

The news circulated in August that President Truman had announced that an atomic bomb had been dropped on Japan. "What kinda bum is dat for Chroist's sake?" someone asked. No one knew what an atomic bomb was. We watched our bulletin board anxiously and read the news release posted there each day. The second atomic bomb was dropped and rumors spread that the Japanese might surrender. I did not know a single veteran who believed it, though. "The Nips won't surrender. We'll have to go back into the islands and wipe 'em all out just like Peleliu. Even if they do surrender in Tokyo, we'll have to fight 'em for years until every last one is knocked off," said a tent mate of mine as we sat around speculating about our future. "Yeah, they might throw in the towel to keep their cities from being bombed flat, but those bypassed Nip troops on Truk, Rabaul, and other places are not going to surrender," added another. I agreed.

Finally, the news came that Japanese peace envoys flying in on one of their bombers were to be escorted into Ie Shima, an island just offshore of northern Okinawa, by a group of U.S. P-38 fighter planes with special green stripes identifying them. Many of us kept our eyes peeled toward Ie Shima and saw this historic event take place—but we still didn't believe the enemy would surrender.

After several days of unbearable suspense, on 14 August 1945 it was announced that the Japanese would surrender unconditionally—the war was over!

It is difficult to express how I felt upon hearing this news. I had a feeling it wasn't true—the war wasn't really over. Most of the veterans felt the same way. We simply sat around and talked quietly, trying to get used to the idea of peace at last. I think we were actually afraid to believe it was true. The First Marine Division had been through too much for too long not to be skeptical. A few new men whooped and shouted, and we heard firearms discharged by celebrating service troops somewhere to the south. But in our camp the men just sat around quietly; most of us felt it was too solemn an occasion to celebrate. The memory of so many dead friends was still fresh in our minds. We heard later that wild celebrations had taken place on V-J Day back in the States and on such big bases as the Philippines. The civilians and the rear echelon might have gone wild, but the prevailing attitude among my comrades was a mixture of quiet relief and disbelief.

We were kept busy during these eventful days on working parties to shape up our camp area. One of the most memorable working parties I was on during camp construction had the job of clearing a dense growth of yucca plants from an area that had been designated for officer's country. This was a narrow strip of uncultivated ground about twenty feet wide, shaded by huge pines. One warm clear day about ten of us began chopping down and clearing the yucca plants with picks and axes so some officers' tents could be pitched in the shade of the pines. No sooner had we chopped out the yucca plants bordering the impenetrable thicket, bristling with leaves tipped with needle-sharp spines, than we discovered that the area was the dumping ground for rocks and other debris when the area farmers cleared their agricultural fields. This made it very hard going to cut and dig out the yucca plants. We also soon discovered the rocky ground was a haven for snakes. There were two species of snakes on Okinawa, one poisonous and the other nonpoisonous. We were ordered to kill all snakes, cut off the head about three inches behind the neck, and turn them over to a corpsman who had a chart to identify the two species.

By midafternoon, when our working party secured their tools for the day, we had cleared an area about thirty-eight feet long and killed over twenty snakes. It was backbreaking work chopping the yucca, and every time someone spotted a snake, we all had to stop and help kill the reptile. Fortunately, no one was bitten. The men voiced many profane, and profound, comments regarding our having to clear a place for officers' tents that was so snake-infested. We later heard that about half the snakes we killed were the poisonous species.

However, enlisted men, particularly veterans, had subtle ways of getting their revenge without revealing any apparent breach of discipline. Our tent camp was built on the edge of a high cliff overlooking the sea. Not long after we had settled into our tents, the first big storm hit us. We had all tightened and adjusted our tent ropes and "battened down the hatches" as the saying went, and we sat on our cots to ride it out. The wind roared in unobstructed straight off the sea and gusted with a force of at least forty to fifty mph. We peered out from under our swaying tents at the sheets of rain driven before the gale and could barely see the tents across the company street. Our ropes held, and our drainage ditches carried off the little rivers made by the torrent. I was just musing about the luxury of a dry tent and a cot to sack out in instead of a flooded foxhole when someone shouted above the gale: "OK you guys. Outside! You are on a working party to report to the company office—on the double." "Oh no!" groaned someone. "Dammit to hell—what kinda screwed up detail is this?" growled someone else. Discipline being what it was, one obeyed orders immediately or was made to wish he had. We tumbled out into the storm clad only in khaki shorts, boondockers, and fatigue caps or helmet liners. Cpl. R. V. Burgin had recovered from his wound and returned from the hospital and was in charge of the working party. Cursing and grumbling, we trudged behind him through the deluge up to the company office tent. We stood around in the company street with rain pouring down on us while a senior NCO in the tent told Burgin to have us adjust the ropes on the tent directly across from the company office.

"OK boys, let's go," said Burgin, who was as disgusted as we were. We sullenly shuffled across to the tent, which was swaying violently in the high wind. Unless the ropes were adjusted, it was obvious that it would soon be blown over. The five or six of us turned to and began to adjust the ropes. Someone peeped inside and then passed the word to the rest of us that the tent was occupied by four brand-new replacement second lieutenants fresh from the States. They had just come into 3/5 and hadn't even been assigned to tents in officer's country yet because of the storm.

This was hard to take—working in the pouring rain to adjust a tent for four shavetails who had just come overseas. When I thought of all the rain we had endured during the recent campaign, it made me boil. We all felt the same way. I looked at Burgin and saw him carefully signaling to us. George and I were on the windward side of the tent tugging on the ropes to hold the tent steady. Burgin's signals were unmistakable. But I could scarcely believe he intended for us to do it! However, when he gave the signal, we released the ropes. The tent, of course, blew over immediately. There sat four astonished new lieutenants dressed in starched khakis sitting on their sacks.

The deluge drenched them in an instant. "Teehut!" yelled Burgin as he saluted the officers—their new gold bars shining on their now soaked shirt collars. We all popped to rigid attention and saluted smartly. The soaked lieutenants arose awkwardly from their previously dry cots and returned our salutes. They were embarrassed and totally unprepared for this development. It was pitiful, yet comical, to see them trying to maintain their official decorum as the wind howled around the flapping tent and the downpour swept across them and all their cots, uniforms, and gear. "Terribly sorry, Suh!" shouted Burgin as he saluted the nearest officer. "That's all right—carry on," said the befuddled lieutenant as he returned the salute. Then with faked ferocity and fury, Burgin yelled at us, "OK you guys, let's get this heah tent squared away. Don't just stand theah, move, move!" Barely able to suppress our laughter, we bustled around giving the impression of working diligently to get the tent back up against the wind and rain. When we finally got everything squared away and battened down, we reported this to the new officers who were inside examining the extent of their soaking. Dismissed, we walked back through the storm to our tent. We had a spring in our stride and laughed all the way. "Boy, did you see the looks on them officers' faces when that rain hit 'em?" laughed one man. "Yeah, it sure wet all their gear all right—they didn't know whether to get mad or laugh." "It'd be our ass if they knew we done that on purpose," a mortarman said as we dried off and hung our soaked shorts up to dry in our tent. "You said that right, and they'd bust you and have your stripes too," I said, turning to Burgin. He just grinned, totally unconcerned. It was actually a mean trick we had played, but, after all, it would help make the new officers salty, someone mused.

We had plenty of leisure time and were allowed a lot of time to rest. A small tent with open flaps was placed at the cliff's edge, overlooking the sea. There were several tables and benches and a big wooden box of books there. This was our library. I spent a lot of time reading there, with the fresh, cool sea breeze and the pounding of the surf below the cliff making it one of the most appreciated libraries I have ever known. I remember completely losing myself in *Wuthering Heights* and several fine historical novels about Colonial America.

When the sea was calm, we went down to the beach at the foot of the cliff and swam in the beautiful pools in the coral reef. There were myriads of forms of aquatic creatures inhabiting the shallows. We saw many exotically colored species of small fishes that were to become popular in the States years later when salt water aquaria were perfected for the home hobbyist.

We enjoyed nightly movies in the regimental theater. There were no coconut logs to sit on "à la Pavuvu," but the screen was placed so we sat on the grassy slope of a steep hill and had a perfect view. Before the picture show would commence, a buddy and I would lie on our backs and watch the numerous shooting stars and marvel at their beauty. We agreed that the stars and moon—in fact, everything—seemed more beautiful than ever before because the war was really over. When the movie ended and the men got up and started back to their respective tents, I always had a feeling of disbelief that the world was at peace and that the mental escape provided by the movie was not just temporary as it had been on Pavuvu. We could really continue to dream of home and not be depressed by that uncertainty of the "next blitz" always in the back of our minds.

There was a great deal of scuttlebutt going around concerning the division's future. Wounded were returning from hospitals every few days, and old men were rotating back to the

States. The most oft-repeated rumor, and probably the most outlandish, was that the entire First Marine Division was to be flown in a huge fleet of B-29s back to the States, each man issued dress blues, and then we would have a victory parade down Fifth Avenue in New York City. The more we talked about it, the more logical it seemed to us in our mental state of wishful thinking. After all, our division had spearheaded the long Pacific counteroffensive, beginning at Guadalcanal, and had gone on to make an outstanding combat record at Cape Gloucester and Peleliu, culminating with Okinawa. Finally, though, reason crept in and chased happy fantasy away. We all made wry jokes about parading down Fifth Avenue "in dress blues and tennis shoes." We knew we would "never get outta the boondocks," as one buddy expressed it.

The next rumor had our division parading down the streets of Tokyo as conquering heroes. Regardless of the fact that some officers, and enlisted men as well, may have thought this very appropriate, many of us just wanted to go home. Personally, I had seen enough of what came out of Japan, so I had absolutely no desire to go there, even though the war was over. One factor that convinced us we would go to Japan was our knowledge of the plans to invade the Japanese home islands. We had been told that in the fall of 1945 three Marine divisions would spearhead the invasion of Kyushu, the southernmost island, followed by several army divisions. The First Marine Division was scheduled to invade Honshu, the largest island. We were to assault the beaches at Yokosuka Naval Base at the mouth of Tokyo Bay and fight on into the Japanese capital. This, we reckoned, would be the hottest spot in the whole invasion of Japan. That the whole business would have been a massive bloodletting was obvious to all of us.

Needless to say, our relief was immense when all of these

plans were abandoned with the Japanese surrender. Nevertheless, we were sure we would still be sent to Japan, but as part of
the occupation forces. When the word was passed that North
China was our destination, most of us were delighted—if we
couldn't go home, China was preferable to Japan. "Hey, you
guys, we'll be China Marines, yeehaw!" shouted a tent mate
when the word was official. The Marine Corps had strong traditional ties with China Duty in Peking, Shanghai, and other
areas. In our division we had a sprinkling of officers and old
regulars who had served there in prewar years, so China Duty
became the constant topic of conversation.

During September, each man received a series of inoculations against cholera and other diseases we might encounter in
China. Everyone hated "the needle." So several of us devised a
plan to put on an act for the "benefit" of the newest replacements. We began to spread the word that the shots they had
received Stateside were nothing compared to the excruciating
pain of inoculations given to us overseas. We described in gory
detail how even the toughest men, some who had been wounded twice in combat, emerged from the sickbay tent with bloody
arms and passed out after their inoculations. We really did a
thorough job of "smokestacking" (fooling) the new men. When
the day came around for K Company to fall out for shots, most
of the new men looked so apprehensive about it that they
looked like they were expecting to "hit the beach." We entered
the sickbay tent on one side in single file, walked through after
getting our shots, and left through the other side. A couple of
corpsmen were cooperating with us in our scheme. After
administering the shots, they sprinkled streaks of tincture of
methiolate down both our arms. Each of us then emerged from
the tent, took a few tottering steps, groaned loudly, and col-
lapsed onto the deck. The effect was stunning on the new men.

After seeing five or six combat veterans come reeling out on the deck, the poor replacements were wide-eyed. Big, muscular "Tex" Barrow, who had recently returned from the hospital after recovering from the gunshot would in the side he received at Kunishi Ridge, put on a particularly convincing performance. "Jeez, did ya see what them shots did to Tex?" I overheard an amazed replacement gasp. One of my fellow conspirators, no longer able to contain his amusement as he lay prostrate by the sickbay entrance, burst out guffawing and laughing. We all got to our feet and joined the chorus of laughter. The "beneficiaries" of our act began to protest loudly that they knew all the time what we had been up to—nonetheless, they appeared greatly relieved upon discovering it was all a joke. Then they stalked jauntily into sickbay and took their shots without flinching.

THE TYPHOON

Some days later, a working party was formed to board ship and stow the battalion's equipment when it came aboard. There were about fifteen of us with an NCO in charge. We were ordered to take all our gear because we would remain aboard ship after the loading. The rest of the troops of our battalion would later embark and we would shove off for China.

The weather was clear and warm. The wind was up, but it usually was on Okinawa. After a short truck ride, we arrived at a beach and boarded a Higgins boat. Our boat headed for one of several APAs (attack transports) anchored offshore. We came alongside and climbed up the cargo net to the main deck. Our NCO directed us to a troop compartment on the main deck forward. After throwing our gear on our racks, we went back out topside to look the ship over. An APA was a large troopship, and this one, the name of which I have forgotten, was either new or it was kept very ship-shape because it was as clean and squared away as any I ever saw. We were given free run of the ship—except officer's country, of course—and had a pleasant time looking around and talking to the crew. "Chow down" was announced, and we ate fine chow in a galley that looked empty with so few Marines in it.

"Now hear this, now hear this," said a voice over the squawk box. "Stand by special sea detail. All hands prepare to get underway immediately." Several buddies and I were topside forward as sailors started scurrying all over the place. "What's the hot dope?" I asked a seaman as he hurried by toward an anchor winch. "Radio reports a big typhoon headed this way. We've got to lift the hook and head for open sea!" "What about us," said one of my buddies. None of the busy sailors answered him. "Gosh, we need to get ashore on the double," another Marine chimed in.

We located our NCO, and he told us that we had orders to remain aboard ship. The storm was so large and coming toward Okinawa so rapidly that all ships had orders to weigh anchor and get under way without a moment's delay. They didn't even have time to let our small working party debark, he said. We knew that typhoons were often so powerful that they could drive even a large troopship ashore and smash it or sink it. The ship could not weather the storm at anchor next to the beach but must ride it out in the open sea. I had seen enough of hurricane damage in Mobile and the Gulf Coast to wish we were now elsewhere. The crew rapidly weighed anchor and the ship got under way. Other ships that had been calmly anchored nearby did likewise with equal haste.

Very soon after leaving our anchorage, the sea got rough, the sky darkened, and the wind blew up stronger. In a few hours we were in the roughest weather I ever experienced at sea. The white caps on the waves were skimmed off by the wind as it blew harder and howled and shrieked through the rigging of the ship. The sea was running high and the ship rolled and pitched violently. When we were in the troughs, I could look up at about a 45-degree angle on either side and see huge walls of water covered with foam and multitudes of waves, crests, and whirlpools. Each time the ship hit a huge wave bow-on, she came down with a splash and shuddered like something alive. Sometimes the propellers must have been out of the water, but we were forward and could not hear them slapping the water, though we could feel the ship vibrating. All hands were ordered below decks because of the danger of being swept overboard.

"Chow down" was announced over the squawk box. We went to the galley by way of companionways, which were just narrow halls, below decks. It was a real test of one's "sea legs" to walk along the companionways even while holding on to the hand rails on each side. One moment the deck receded abruptly from beneath one's feet, but with the next step it heaved up violently and nearly hit one in the face. We finally lurched into the galley, where nearly everything was battened down. The few pots and pans that weren't secured were thrown violently to and fro—as we were served sandwiches and hot joe. We all clutched at tables and hand rails to steady ourselves while we tried to eat and balance the cup of joe in one hand to keep it from sloshing out of the cup. One man forgot and placed his thick china cup on the table, and it instantly went skidding along the table top, hit the bulkhead, and smashed into pieces.

We didn't sleep much that night. Naturally, we were nervous in such a violent storm—even the saltiest sailors aboard were clearly ill at ease. Our biggest problem was now being thrown out of our racks as the ship pitched and tossed.

When morning chow call was sounded, several of us decided, against previously issued orders, to open the hatch onto the main deck and look at the storm. We turned the levers and pushed the heavy metal hatch door slightly open. The wind threw it ajar and we looked aft. Huge waves were breaking over the ship's sides and torrents of sea water were running off the deck. A deluge of rain swept horizontally across the deck, and we could scarcely see the ship's superstructure. The wind was roaring like a locomotive. With great difficulty we pulled the hatch shut against the wind, dogged it down, and never had the slightest desire to reopen it until the storm abated. We did all our subsequent watching through the glass of tightly sealed portholes. As the ship rolled, the view altered between dark sky with torrents of windswept rain and mountainous waves looming up just outside the glass.

Chow was again sandwiches and joe; nothing else could be prepared by the ship's cooks in the galley. I was never more grateful that I was not inclined to seasickness. The men who were, both Marines and navy men, suffered terribly and were quite chagrined over their inability to weather the storm. It could not be helped, though, and no one joked about their misery.

Some of the old navy salts admitted, grudgingly, that this was the worst storm they had ever encountered. It went on for about three days, if I am correct, and on the fourth day the rain stopped and the wind abated. We were allowed topside but told to keep toward the center of the deck and away from the rails— if one was thrown over the side, there was little chance of rescue in such heavy sea. We were told that the ship was returning to the anchorage because the storm had swept across Okinawa and passed on.

There was considerable excitement on deck when we saw through the mist across the huge waves a big U.S. Navy cruiser towing a small vessel by a huge steel cable. How this could be accomplished in such a heavy sea was amazing. "Boy, if that cable snaps she (the smaller vessel) is a goner in this heavy sea," said a sailor. "Yeah, she'd capsize in a minute," observed another. There was much guessing and speculation among the seamen as to the name of the cruiser, but no one knew.

The weather cleared rapidly as we moved back to the anchorage. After the ship anchored, we debarked, were picked up by trucks, and headed back to the battalion's tent camp. The driver said the storm had flattened almost every tent he had seen. He did not exaggerate because evidence of storm damage was everywhere in every encampment of U.S. troops that we passed. It was apparently one of the most powerful typhoons in recent times.

Our battalion area was hardly recognizable. Every tent and frame structure was flat on the ground. Tents were a tangled, tattered mess as men moved about trying to straighten things out. I returned to the site of my tent—it, too, was flat on the ground—and was greeted by my soaked, forlorn tent mates. They had hardly slept since I had left because they had so little shelter from the terrific winds and driving rains. "The only thing that could have made it worse was if we were bein' shelled and shot at like it was at Shuri," said a buddy as he untangled tent ropes from his water-soaked bunk and mattress pad. Altogether, those of us on the working party had not fared so badly after all. However, we agreed we would much rather take any future typhoons ashore. No matter what happened to our tents, it would be mild compared to days and nights of pitching and rolling through mountainous waves aboard a ship that might capsize at any moment.

ON TO NORTH CHINA

Without further developments of note, we boarded ship for China a few days later during the early part of October. One of the sores that had developed on my left hand during the Shuri stalemate in May had never healed, and I now had a case of blood poisoning. So with my left arm in a sling, carrying my gear as best I could, and with the help of buddies, we embarked to become China Marines.

Our voyage from Okinawa was uneventful except for seeing several Japanese floating mines that the ship's 5-inch gunners fired on and detonated. We were all pleased with the coolness of the weather as we headed through the East China Sea and then the Gulf of Chihli. I had to report to sickbay every few hours to soak my hand in a hot solution prepared by a corpsman who did all he could to reduce my discomfort from the blood poisoning in my arm.

After a few days the ship dropped anchor off Taku Bar, where the Hai Ho empties into the Gulf of Chihli. We debarked, transferring to landing craft to cross the bar and unload at the docks of the little town of Taku. The Seventh Marines had previously landed to secure the area, and later various units of service troops came in for their support and supply. We boarded trucks and rode about seven miles to the town of Tangku, which served as the railhead and gateway to the sea for Tientsin, thirty-six miles inland.

At Tangku we boarded a train for Tientsin. All the men were in high spirits and very excited about the prospects of pleasant duty in China. The train was small and lightly built by American standards, and the engine had a shrill whistle, but it was a steam locomotive just the same and belched a huge column of black smoke, hissed, and puffed. Everyone enjoyed this greatly. The cars had wooden seats but were totally lacking in any of those frills or comforts found on American Pullman cars. Glass windows were about the only redeeming factor. There was a head (restroom) at one end of the car I was on. The toilet was the subject of much discussion among the troops—in fact, it was a source of fascination. No one had ever seen anything like it before. There was no seat, and the toilet bowl was recessed into the floor. The user simply placed one foot on each side, flexed his knees, and straddled it to assume the proper position. There was a brass bar along the wall to the front so that one could steady one's self as the train lurched along. The toilet tank for the flushing water was on the wall and operated with a pull chain. At some time in the past, this probably had been operative, but now the odor of the little room indicated it had not had the attentions of a plumber for a considerable time. A lack of all types of maintenance was typical of Chinese trains.

When we boarded the train for Tientsin, everyone was in a happy, carefree mood. The men were waving and shouting greetings to the curious Chinese we saw in the station as the engine puffed and wheezed itself into forward motion. During the entire 300-plus-mile ride, we behaved like a bunch of boys on a weekend outing. Finally, we pulled into the big Tientsin railroad depot, which looked like many older railroad stations I had seen in the States. We were told we could get out and walk up and down outside the cars but were ordered not to leave the trackside area. We talked to several Marines we saw on guard duty in the station. They told us they were members of the First Marines. They vowed that China Duty was "good duty"— at which news we were elated. There were a few Chinese civilians in the station, and although none spoke English, they were sincerely friendly and kept smiling and saying "Ding hao (very good)." It was obvious they were delighted American troops had come to China.

After a brief period I noticed a locomotive engine with one passenger car attached being switched onto our track and backed up close to our engine. There had been a considerable amount of conferring between our 3/5 officers and the Marine officers in the station—something out of the ordinary had obviously developed. "What's the hot dope, Lieutenant?" I asked a K Company officer. "We don't know, but we might run into trouble with the Communists when we enter Peiping," he answered gravely. All, or a portion, of L Company was transferred to the single car pulled by the lead engine. It was evident that most of the company's light machine guns were placed in the car. "All aboard" was the order, and the two trains went huffing and puffing out of the Tientsin station. Our train followed the L Company detachment about one hundred yards to the rear.

Our holiday mood was dampened, and the men were subdued by the news that we might have to fight our way into Peiping—the war was over and we had had our fill of fighting. We were ordered to keep a sharp lookout on the countryside for any signs of trouble. Earlier, we were all issued ammo. If the trains were stopped due to hostile action, we were to load our weapons on the double, get the hell off the train, and deploy and take cover on either side of the track. Thus, our trip from Tientsin to Peiping lost its holiday-excursion atmosphere and was filled with tension and dread as we headed toward what might be more combat. I thought with bitterness of the news reports we had heard concerning demands by U.S. troops in the Pacific, many of the most vociferous being noncombatants, clamoring loudly to be sent home immediately after the Japanese surrendered—and here we were heading into we knew not what. Possibly a new war.

As our train puffed and lurched along, we kept a sharp lookout through the windows. The terrain was quite flat. Everything was windswept, dusty, and brown. Different shades of brown, but brown nevertheless. Windswept, dusty, and brown typified the autumn and winter landscape of North China.

The desolate landscape was divided into small agricultural fields now lying fallow. An occasional house constructed of dirt bricks with a tile roof and surrounded with a dirt wall interrupted the monotony. Some of the dusty roads were lined with leafless trees, and except for these and smaller trees in the farm yards, the countryside was devoid of any vegetation. We passed a field with small dome-shaped mounds, each topped with a piece of white paper weighted down with a dirt clod. An old China Marine said it was a peasant cemetery.

We saw a few peasants moving along the roads quite some distance from the railroad. Every few hundred yards on each side of the railroad, a Chinese soldier was posted on guard. They kept their eyes on the approaches to the track, and I never saw one turn and look at the train. These men were clad in khaki uniforms, caps, and wrap leggings. Each was armed with a Japanese Arisaka rifle. We were told that they were the puppet-government troops armed and trained by the Japanese. They were responsible for the safety of the railroad.

Our train made at least one stop at a village along route; I assume it was the village of Lang Fang but am not certain. Some of us got off our car and stood around outside. A Chinese guard came up and greeted us. We grinned and tried in vain to communicate. When he saw that my left arm was in a sling, the guard became highly animated. "Oooh, ah, Zhurban boo hao (Japanese very bad)!" he said with a frown. Then he pointed his rifle off into the distance, exclaimed "beng, beng!" and pointed to my arm in the sling. He obviously thought I had been wounded in the arm during the war. "Hey, Sledgehammer, this Chink thinks you're a wounded hero," laughed one of my buddies. We got a big laugh out of the fact that I was one of the few K Company men who didn't have the Purple Heart and this Chinese guard thought I was recovering from a wound inflicted by the Japanese. I tried to explain to him that I had blood poisoning in my arm as a result of a sore on my hand. But it was hopeless—he didn't understand a word of English, and I hadn't yet learned any Chinese. The more I attempted to explain the infection, the more convinced he seemed to be of the severity of the wound, and he cursed the Japanese volubly in Chinese. Finally, the train pulled out with the Chinese sentry gently patting my "wounded" arm and shaking his head sadly. We made a couple of other stops, and every Chinese soldier, civilian, and railroad man I encountered treated me with great deference, pointing to my arm and growling angrily, "Zhurban boo hao!" I finally gave up trying to explain blood poisoning in English to Chinese-speaking people and just repeated "Zhurban boo hao!"

Without any opposition or mishap, our train entered the huge rail yard at Peiping and pulled into the station. To our delight the trackside was lined with Chinese schoolchildren holding little American flags and waving and smiling at us. Our senior officers got off the train and were greeted by Peiping city officials and a couple of European nurses. We detrained and moved amid crowds of cheering Chinese out of the station to a street where we boarded Marine trucks that had preceded us to Peiping. My arm in its sling continued to be a source of awe to the Chinese and elicited many manifestations of sympathy from them—much to the amusement of my many buddies who had been wounded during the war.

The concern about, and precautions against, Communist opposition to our entrance into Peiping were all well grounded. Brig. Gen. William A. Worton, USMC, had gone to North China with an advance party to make certain arrangements for the Marine occupation before we set sail from Okinawa. When it became known that Marines would occupy Peiping, Communist officers requested a meeting with Worton.

General Worton met in Peiping with Chinese Communist

general Chou En-lai. Chou stated that he agreed to U.S. occupation of Tientsin but that Communist troops would fight to prevent Marines from occupying Peiping. Worton told Chou that the Marines would definitely occupy the city as planned. He also told the Communist leader that Marines were ready and combat-experienced, had overwhelming air support, and would drive straight through anything the Communists put in their way. The stormy session ended inconclusively. The Communists were apparently resigned to U.S. occupation of Tientsin, Tangku, and Chinwangtao in Hopeh Province (by the First Marine Division) as well as Tsingtao on the Shantung Peninsula (by the Sixth Marine Division) to repatriate the Japanese. However, they were bitterly opposed to our entering Peiping, which they wanted for themselves.

Peiping had been China's capital for about seven hundred years and was a symbol of national power and the cultural and educational center of North China. Peiping was to Chinese culture what Paris is to French culture. If Marines entered the ancient city, it meant they would not just repatriate Japanese there but also hold the city until the arrival from the south of Chinese Nationalist Forces under Chiang Kai-shek. This the Communists wanted to prevent in order to take Peiping under their own control.

We in the ranks knew little of this at the time, but we breathed easier after safely entering Peiping and receiving such a rousing welcome. The first building we saw as we detrained was the imposing ancient multistory tower of the Chien Men Gate. It stood like a massive fortress atop the huge centuries-old wall around the city. Chien Men was a focal point of Peiping.

Our trucks moved out, at a rather rapid pace, and sped through miles of Peiping's streets. Huge crowds of people packed both sides of our route all the way. They held American flags, waved, smiled, and shouted, "Ding hao (very good)!" until it was deafening. We sat or stood in our open trucks and waved and shouted. Jim put more into it than anyone in our truck. He stood the entire time and shook his fist exultantly at the sky and shouted, "Gung ho (work together)!" until he was red in the face. The ridiculous thing was that "Gung ho," the only Chinese he knew, was the Communist army slogan. The slogan had been adopted early in the war by the Second Marine Raider Battalion long before anyone thought American and Communist interests would clash. When the Marine raider battalions were disbanded and the men incorporated into regular Marine infantry battalions, the term "Gung ho" took on a slightly different connotation from "work together." To say a Marine was "Gung ho" meant that he was eager and willing to excel and follow orders almost to the extreme—that is, he was an "eager beaver." When Jim yelled "Gung ho" amid all the noise, the crowds around the truck thought he was yelling "Ding hao" and responded loudly with "Ding hao"—at last, an American who could greet them in Chinese! Jim was too worked up and excited to listen to our explanation of what was happening and yelled "Gung ho" until he was hoarse. I have often thought how bewildered those Peiping citizens would have been had they realized that this exuberant Marine was not shouting a polite greeting to them but a Communist slogan—a slogan of the very people against whom we had come to protect their city. But there was so much yelling and cheering no one could hear what Jim was shouting—it was his enthusiasm the Chinese liked.

How far our parade went and how long it lasted I do not know, but throngs of people surged into the streets to shake our hands and show their pro-American sentiments. The Chinese police kept them out of the path of our trucks with difficulty.

People crowded the windows and roofs of buildings along our route. It was truly a "victory parade" for us, and we enjoyed it immensely. We hadn't seen civilization for a long time.

Finally, the trucks entered the Legation Quarter and stopped by the Italian Legation. The only thing that prevented our reception to Peiping from being perfect was the large number of carefully hand-painted signs posted about reading, "Welcome U.S. Army." This was a real cause for much "beating of gums and chipping of teeth" among a trainload of veteran U.S. Marines.

We were moved into the Italian Legation until further orders. The place was beautiful, with large marble columns on many buildings and striking marble floors inside. A stone wall for defense, containing firing posts for rifles and machine guns and topped with barbed wire, surrounded the legation compound. I found out later that most of the foreign legations were constructed this way for protection during China's politically turbulent past. There were a few Italian civilians around who had recently been released from internment by the Japanese. We talked with a handsome young Italian boy about fourteen years old who spoke perfect English. One of my buddies from Brooklyn, who was a first-generation Italian American, began speaking to the boy. After a few sentences, he turned to us in amazement. "Hey youse goys, dis kid speaks bettah eyetalian dan oy do, for Chroist's sake!" he exclaimed. Another Marine jokingly poked him in the ribs and said, "Aw, you dumb wop, he speaks better *English* than you do, too." Everyone laughed, but he grudgingly accepted the fact that literacy was not confined to New Yorkers.

After a couple of hours, we were ordered to move out to the English Legation, where 3/5 would be billeted. Outside in the street, a character walked up and introduced himself to some of us as Val. He told us he had been raised in North China after his parents, who were Czarist sympathizers, fled Russia during the revolution. Val was about my size, a blue-eyed blond with a thin mustache. He wore a nondescript khaki uniform and a small automatic pistol in a holster on his belt. The incredible thing about him was that he spoke English with an accent more Brooklynese than our buddies who were natives of Brooklyn, New York. Val told me he had learned English from Americans stationed on an airfield in South China, but his answers to all my other questions about himself were evasive and vague. He seemed more interested in getting to know us and, though acting the part of a "buddy" welcoming us to Peiping, he was constantly questioning us about what our duties would be in the area. This overwhelming interest in our duties seemed strange in view of the fact that he claimed to be a railroad policeman for the Chinese Nationalist government. From our first meeting until the day I left Peiping, I was convinced that Val was a spy for the Chinese Communists. If he was anything for certain, Val was one of the cockiest men I ever knew. Also, he showed his utmost contempt for the Chinese by constantly ranting and raving and claiming that they were all stupid and inferior. (Actually, Val was not particularly intelligent himself—he just had a big mouth.)

I found that Val was not unique among Russians in Peiping in his attitude. Every Russian I met there was scornful of the Chinese. Their attitude was only matched by the deep distrust and dislike felt by the Chinese for the Russians.

We were soon billeted in the English Legation. The old two-story British barracks was not large enough to accommodate our entire battalion, so some men were billeted in the houses of former British officials. The mortar section occupied two rooms of a comfortable brick bungalow within the legation walls. Another K Company platoon was billeted in the other rooms. All of the former residents' furniture had been taken by the Japanese, so our sole furnishings were wooden bunks placed in the rooms to form squad bays. The bunks were Japanese army bunks hinged across the middle so that after the bedding was folded, the foot end of the bunk could be folded back over the head end, thus taking up less floor space. Even with our bed rolls on these bunks, they were mighty hard as beds. Someone commented that it was no wonder the Japanese troops were so damn tough if they had to sleep on such bunks as these. However, we didn't complain. This was the first time I had slept in a house with a roof over my head and a wooden floor beneath my feet since leaving Camp Elliot nearly two years before. Other than certain periods in tents and aboard ship, the open sky was the only roof many of us had known for a long time—we had slept on, or in, the ground more than in bunks. I actually had to become accustomed to sleeping indoors again.

The English Legation, or "Engua Foo" as the Chinese called it—all legations were called "Foo" because the word indicated a walled-in compound—was extremely interesting. Living there gave one the feeling of being in the late nineteenth century. To me the place seemed haunted by the spirit of Rudyard Kipling. Although not ornate like its Italian counterpart, the English Legation was spacious and laid out with attractive gardens and substantial buildings and walls of red brick. One could see evidence of repairs on the walls from damage during the Boxer Rebellion in 1899. Many Europeans had been besieged in Engua Foo. The relief column of foreign troops, containing several battalions of U.S. Marines, had broken the siege after heavy fighting. The Marines had particularly distinguished themselves in the fight.

Within the legation walls there were shops for every type of artisan—carpenter, blacksmith, tailor, cobbler, and others. The

Chinese were allowed once more to set up business in these shops. It amazed me to watch them fashion a pair of dress shoes out of pieces of leather or a jacket out of a Marine blanket. As a boy I had watched a blacksmith shoe my horse and repair wooden wagon wheels, and I also had seen a tailor alter clothing, but the skill and patience of the Chinese craftsmen surpassed anything I ever saw before or since.

After we got settled, the first thing on the mind of every Marine I knew was non-G.I. food—women came second. Regular chowtime was announced and food served in the spacious, high-ceilinged British mess hall. Much to our disgust, for seven days it consisted of C-rations served out by battalion cooks. The only dinner and supper variation from this was "Corn Willy" (corned-beef hash), which was worse than C-rations. Most of my buddies usually ate most of their food in one of the many restaurants when we went out on liberty in the city. Even at a later period when our galley had beef and fresh vegetables to prepare, we still preferred restaurants. "Them cooks is bettah as stretcher bearers than they is as cooks—they can ruin any kinda chow when they cook it," observed one veteran.

The blood poisoning in my arm cleared up a few days after settling into our billets in Peiping. I was glad to be rid of the infection as well as the sling, even though it had brought forth endless expressions of sympathy from the Chinese.

A WHOLE NEW WORLD

One of the legendary benefits to Marines serving on peacetime duty stations in the Far East was the privilege of hiring servants, or "houseboys," as they were known. Houseboys could wash clothes, shine shoes, run errands, and do almost any job for us but clean or handle our weapons—that was strictly against orders. The mortar section houseboy was a young Chinese named Hao Ching Fu. Hao was about twenty years old and about my size. He could not speak a single word of English when he came to the legation to work for us. So I set about teaching him English, and he taught me a good deal of Chinese. He turned out to be the more accomplished linguist, I must admit, although I did learn enough Chinese to get along with the merchants and rickshaw boys.

Hao was very likable and was referred to by my buddies as "that Chink that speaks English with an Alabama accent." Hao, like most Chinese, called all Americans "Joe"—except me. He always addressed me by my "Chinese name," Ee Jen Sheh. This was as close as the Chinese artisan who made brass name stamps could come to Eugene Sledge. After I pronounced my name once, the man looked puzzled, but then he said slowly: "Ah so, Ee Jen Sheh. Such is your name in Chinese." "How do you translate it?" I asked. "It means gorden schorar," he answered with a broad smile of satisfaction. "Golden Scholar!" I remarked in amazement. "Yes, it is so," he replied. This provided my buddies an unending source for kidding me—but Hao took it seriously.

Hao went with me on liberty several times and was a fine guide to Peiping's historic sites. But his working hours were such that he could not get off when I could. So when I had no duty, we would spend hours sitting on my bunk pouring over a little paperback book with Chinese phrases translated and written phonetically for English-speaking people. I could write my name in Chinese characters, but I soon gave up with other words and was resigned to being illiterate in the written language. Our language lessons were often interrupted when Hao had to run an errand or shine someone's shoes—but that was his job and there was no more cheerful, industrious houseboy than Hao. He and I became very close friends. I was curious about Buddhism and asked him about it. Religion was the one subject he absolutely would not discuss, though. I rather suspect that this was because of some fear on his part that a Christian might laugh at him or perhaps try to convert him. I had no intention of doing either, but, nevertheless, Chinese religion was the one subject that Hao would not talk with me about. His long, blue cloth, rabbit-fur-lined robe was eternally spotless, his hair was short and neat, and his fingernails as clean as those of any Marine at inspection. Hao was as clean-living and clean-minded as his appearance. He and I both had tears in our eyes when I left Peiping to return home. I have often wondered what sort of treatment he received at the hands of the Communists when they took over Peiping. The fact that Hao had worked as a houseboy for U.S. Marines during the occupation probably did not help him with that ruthless regime.

During the first few days we were in Peiping, a rickshaw ride anywhere in that large city cost the equivalent of three cents in American money. However, when the astute Chinese quickly learned how rich a Marine private was, with his sixty-dollar-a-month salary, compared to the average citizen of Peiping, the price of a ride jumped to "five gold" almost overnight. (One U.S. dollar was referred to as "one gold.") Colonel Frisbie, the regimental CO of the Fifth Marines, was said to be an old "China hand" and knew how to deal with the Chinese. The order came out that no Marine was to ride a rickshaw until further notice. We grumbled, but when we went out of the legation on liberty, we knew we had better walk. The rickshaw coolies became frantic after a day or so. ("Coolie" was the name given to all civilian laborers in China.) They crowded around each Marine as he walked out of the gate, shouting "You want a rickshaw, Joe!" We simply shook our heads and walked on. I would yell "Tai kway (too dear or expensive)!" The coolies were persistent and would trot behind us pulling their empty vehicles. After a few days the price of a ride was set at five to fifteen cents American money, depending on the distance. This was certainly fair enough—no human being, or beast of burden, ever worked harder for his livelihood than a rickshaw coolie. The ban on Marines' riding in rickshaws was lifted, much to the delight of all concerned.

Each morning our battalion cooks over in the British mess hall prepared a breakfast of slabs of fried Spam (that loaf-shaped canned meat heartily detested by all) and scrambled dehydrated eggs. Like all dehydrated foods then, the eggs had an extremely unpalatable aftertaste. Some mornings there were few takers. I suppose most of the other men of 3/5 were breakfasting in a similar fashion to my buddies and me.

Early each morning, Hao Ching Fu would appear laden with packages of fresh bacon, fresh eggs, and loaves of French bread, purchased with money we had sent him home with the previous night. He would take our mess kits and the food out to the kitchen in a backyard outbuilding connected to the house by a covered walkway. There he would fix us a breakfast fit for a king. It was common for me to eat six or seven pieces of bacon and six to eight eggs. Other men ate even more—we were literally "out of our heads" on the subject of fresh food. Hao cleaned up and squared away everything after we ate. We usually ate noon chow in the chow hall. When we had liberty in the evening we ate in restaurants. When we had guard duty or stand by, we arranged for a buddy on liberty to bring in prepared food of some sort from a restaurant. Our preoccupation with food may seem odd, but most of us had not eaten fresh food of any type in nearly two years or more. There was very little in the way of refrigerated food in the Pacific War except on ships. But on troop transports the sailors were served the fresh foods while we got spam, dehydrated eggs, and dehydrated potatoes. Even copious amounts of tomato ketchup could not mask the synthetic aftertaste of the dehydrated foods we were given.

During the early days on liberty in Peiping, most men I knew were primarily interested in good food and sightseeing. Prior to shipping out from Okinawa, we had been shown some rather vivid Navy Medical Corps films about the perils of venereal disease. Consequently, most of the troops steered a wide course around Peiping's red-light district, where venereal disease was said to be rampant. In the early days, too, the men were simply so awed by the fact that they were back in civilization that many of them had little inclination to carouse. Inevitably things changed. We settled down to our routine of guard duty and patrols in and around the city. The novelty of sightseeing wore off gradually, and the men began drinking. There was nothing like a man being "three sheets to the wind" to make him forget all the lectures and warnings about venereal disease. As a result, the number of cases of gonorrhea began to increase. So there were additional lectures about VD prevention and the warning was passed around that a man would have his pay docked for any days missed due to a VD infection. The men responded to this by taking the sulfur tablets in their combat first-aid kits in an effort to control their infections. Sickbay said this was an ineffective treatment; then the new policy was that men would not be punished for having VD. Instead, when we checked in at the gate after liberty, we now had to report "exposed" or "unexposed" to the possibility of infection. As we entered the gate, we filed past a table where an NCO checked each man's name by the light of a small lamp. No one seemed to have any inclination to deny it if he had been with a woman while on liberty. The men all knew it was for their own protection.

One day while walking across the parade ground in front of the barracks, I passed "Lt. Mac." I had not seen him for some time, for he no longer commanded our mortar section (a fact that had raised our morale to great heights). We were glad to be free of him. "One Grease Ball" had recovered from the wounds he received on Okinawa and was now our mortar section officer. We all liked him a great deal. Unlike Mac, he was an officer we could respect. I saluted Mac smartly as we passed and said, "Hello, Mac," addressing him by his code name out of sheer habit. "Halt!" ordered Mac. I halted and stood stiffly at attention. Mac walked around in front of me and said "Sledgehammer, the war is over. Cut out this Mac stuff and address me as Lt. ———." "Yessir, Lieutenant," I replied, admitting to myself that he was correct and I had erred in not observing the proper courtesy due to an officer.

I remained at attention expecting Mac to dismiss me. He didn't, though. He had something he had to unload from his petty little mind before he dismissed me. He had to assert his authority. Mac looked at me with a supercilious sneer and proceeded to tell me that in checking over the liberty lists, he had noticed that I always reported in "unexposed." (It occurred to me that his duties must not be particularly demanding if he had either the time or inclination to study the sexual habits of the troops. After all, he was not a medical officer.) "Are your reports correct?" he asked. "Yessir," I answered. "Why?" he said. "Why, sir?" I replied in disbelief. "Yes, why are you always unexposed?" he hissed. "Because, sir, I don't want to get VD," I replied. (My moral convictions were none of his business.) "I do not believe that. Aren't you a man?" he scoffed. "Sir, no one ever questioned *my* manhood in combat on *Peleliu,* or on *Okinawa,*" I shot back, as I struggled to maintain self-control. That remark struck him like a verbal vertical butt stroke to the chin. His face flushed. "Knock if off, or I'll run you up for insubordination. Dismissed!" he snapped. I saluted, said, "Yessir," and went on my way. My mind was racing with two inner voices: one proclaiming what an incredible fool he was for being an officer and scoffing at a man for avoiding infection, and the other cursing him with the finest, most polished, most elaborate Marine Corps profanity (which is equivalent to fourth-year Latin in its complexity)—it would have been admirable coming from the lips of a salty first sergeant with thirty years in the Corps, if I must say so.

It had been a close call. Mac had been looking for trouble, and if I had 1 lost my self-control I would have landed in the brig. That would have delayed my returning home for an indeterminate period of time. It would also have spoiled my perfect conduct record. He had pulled rank on me and tried to humiliate me, but I pulled my two battle stars on him (he hadn't been on Peleliu). He knew I had bested him and he was furious. Mac had not forgotten the way we laughed at him and called his bluff on Okinawa 1 May to fulfill his oft-repeated pledge to charge the Japanese lines with kabar and .45-caliber pistol the first time a K Company man got killed. As I described in *With the Old Breed*, when Howard Nease and Private Westbrook were machine gunned, Mac reacted vigorously by digging in like a badger—charging the enemy was the farthest thing from his mind, and we had kidded him then for digging so deeply.

In sharp contrast to Lt. Mac, it would have been unheard of for any other of our officers in China to have spoken to an enlisted man the way he spoke to me. As for my fellow veteran enlisted buddies, their attitude concerning a man's behavior on liberty was one of complete tolerance. What he did or did not do was his own personal business. If one wanted to drink like a fish, raise unholy hell, and carouse, they often remarked about what a "wildcat" he was on liberty. If another went out, had a beer or two, and then went on his way while the wildcats went carousing—that, too, was OK as long as they were not "preached to" about their wild habits. Our friendships forged in combat resulted in our tolerating each other's personal habits and behavior on liberty. We might make light jokes about it, but the old hands respected each other too much to scoff at a man because of his moral choices. Combat veterans did not feel the need to raise hell on liberty to "prove themselves." If they raised hell, it was because they wanted to, and if they didn't drink and womanize, that was their choice.

In the afternoon on 19 October 1945, we held a parade on the Tung Tan Glacis. This was a large open area bordered by Hatamen Street on the east and some of the foreign legations on the west. It was the first Marine parade held in Peiping since 1941. We wore helmets, pressed dungarees, and leggings and carried our weapons. We passed in review for a Chinese general and a U.S. diplomat from Washington. The parade was heralded with many complimentary statements in an article in the English-language newspaper, *Peiping Chronicle.* Our tanks, artillery, and vehicles were freshly painted field green and were wiped with a thin film of oil so that they glistened in the bright sun. The troops looked sharp and squared away and paraded with absolute precision. A few old-time salts said we were a credit to "the Old Corps." I must admit we were pleased with our precision and appearance.

I didn't particularly enjoy parades, but it did occur to me that day that my buddies paraded as impressively as they fought. I had a premonition that I would never cease being deeply proud of serving in the Fifth Marines. It was hard to believe we had once looked so filthy and bedraggled in the steaming heat on Peleliu's rugged ridges and in the corpse-reeking morass at Shuri, Okinawa. At the parade during a period "at rest," I talked to some of the Europeans and English-speaking Chinese nearby in the large crowd gathered to view the ceremony. It was with a sense of gratification that I noted they were fully aware of our division's combat record in the Pacific. It amazed me that they knew about the battles of Peleliu and Okinawa— we were not looked on as "parade ground" troops but as conquerors of Japan's toughest soldiers. These civilians were glad to have an American combat division such as ours in North China, and they frankly told us so. They knew that we had the firepower and the experience to keep the various marauding bands at bay. But it was a hell of a dangerous situation—some "peace."

During October, the weather grew increasingly chilly. The scuttlebutt was that we would receive our dress greens, which were wool, any day. In the meantime, we wore khakis and field jackets on liberty and dungarees on duty in the legation and working parties. Since our long months in the Pacific and tropics had not conditioned us to withstand the chill winds of October in North China, we spent some miserable hours on guard duty about the legation and on parade.

As cold weather descended in November, we were delighted to receive our winter-service greens. Uniforms mean a great deal to Marines. Our uniforms were uniquely Marine Corps. We had no back pockets in either khaki or wool green trousers. "Bulging pockets ain't in keeping with a sharp, squared away uniform," was the way an old salty instructor at Camp Elliott had explained the absence of hip pockets on Marine trousers. We wore the green wool overseas cap in China because the barracks hat (or hat with frame and leather bill) was too bulky to ship in a sea bag. The overseas cap was warm and could be easily tucked under the belt when not being worn. Our overcoats, much needed in North China, were very thick green wool, double breasted, and patterned after a World War I–type trench coat.

All items of our uniforms had to be tailored, at our own expense, to fit *perfectly*. This was no problem in Peiping, where skillful tailors abounded. From what I saw, if a Marine's uniform wasn't a perfect fit when he stood inspection, either on parade or before going on liberty, he was made to regret it by being assigned EPD (Extra Police Detail) or extra mess duty. It was a forlorn sight to see a man clad in dungarees and boondockers carrying his bucket around the legation grounds policing up cigarette butts, matchsticks, and other trash, looking after his sharply dressed buddies in pressed greens as they went striding out of the gate on liberty. "We'll be thinkin' about you, ole buddy, when we drink a beer," they would say. "Aw, knock it off, you meatheads," would be the disgruntled reply, as the Gunny's words would ring in his ears, "The uniform will be properly tailored and will be worn with pride, and in the correct military manner, at all times."

There was no doubt about it, our greens were fine-looking uniforms. In those days, the U.S. Army troops' O.D. (olive drab) wool uniforms appeared to us to be cheaply constructed of threadbare light brown wool (I never could see that it was olive, but it certainly was drab) that was usually poorly tailored and loose fitting. "I'd sure hate to hafta wear one of them army uniforms, there just ain't no way a guy can look sharp in one of 'em," remarked a buddy as we once watched soldiers walking along the street sightseeing in Peiping.

Even though being back in our dress greens did a lot for our morale, many of us wished for our dress blues. These uniforms were not issued to troops during war years, but while in training many of us purchased them at our own expense from approved uniform suppliers. Before we shipped out for the Pacific, we had boxed up our blues and sent them home to our parents to keep until we returned—if we were lucky and did.

INCIDENT AT LANG FANG

Those of us who were stationed in Peiping had the "good duty," and we knew it. But late in October, a sergeant came into the English Legation, where most of the Fifth Marines were billeted, and announced that a detachment from K Company was scheduled to pull a tour of guard duty. A reinforced rifle platoon with two light machine-gun sections, as well as my 60mm mortar squad, would be sent to protect the division's radio relay station at Lang Fang, which was located along a railroad line midway between Peiping and Tientsin. We received these orders with a noticeable lack of enthusiasm, but we knew we had not been sent to northern China for rest and rehabilitation.

The next morning dawned crisp and clear. Having been issued ammunition and C-rations, our detachment of roughly forty Marines and a corpsman, under the command of a lieutenant, boarded five trucks and a jeep and set out for Lang Fang. After we passed through one of the big tower gates in the huge wall surrounding Peiping, we looked back and saw Chinese soldiers pulling the gate shut behind us. Our convoy went out into the windswept countryside while we kept a sharp lookout for possible Communist ambush. Some miles down the road, we moved through an ancient walled village, virtually unchanged since the time of Kublai Khan and Marco Polo. It was crowded with Chinese peasants. Not a single person could be seen outside the walls—grim evidence of the terrible unrest and chaos infecting the countryside.

We soon arrived at Lang Fang, an unwalled village of about

five hundred people. Our convoy entered a modern walled compound; atop one small building was a radio antenna. Behind the radio station were our quarters in some one-story, wooden, barracks-type buildings. Several of us were detailed for guard duty along the compound wall. My post was on the fire step overlooking a narrow intersection lined with rows of single-story houses of mud and brick. Looking through a fire port and over the parapet, which had barbed wire stretched on top, I realized that we would be easy prey for any snipers in nearby houses.

Several curious Chinese children gathered in the street, and I began talking with them as well as I could, considering my limited knowledge of their language. I tossed a couple of pieces of C-ration candy to them, and they shouted their appreciation. Immediately, a crowd of about fifty people gathered, shouting and holding out their hands. Those of us who were on the wall soon ran out of candy and started tossing hardtack biscuits to them. They begged for more. Then a sergeant double-timed up and told us to save our rations in case we were cut off. (A chilling thought, to be sure!) In late afternoon my buddy and I were relieved by the next watch, and we set out beyond the compound gate in search of fresh eggs.

About a block to our right, we noticed the Japanese camp, which had several imposing brick buildings. Curious about our recent enemy, we went up to its gate, where a sentry snapped to and saluted us. We returned his salute. (All Japanese troops of all ranks saluted all Marines regardless of rank. I was told they respected us because we had defeated the best troops they had.) We entered the camp, knowing from what we had seen in Peiping that the Japanese were now on their best behavior around Americans. An officer invited us to two tables neatly spread with white tablecloths. On one were servings of tea and cookies; on the other were several fine samurai sabers. The officer saluted, bowed, and pointing to the tables said in perfect English, "You are welcome to anything you wish." Just then, another Marine ran up and told us we were not allowed in the Japanese camp yet. The Japanese officer seemed confused by our sudden departure.

Grumbling mightily, we headed back into the village, still in search of eggs. Some Chinese peasants walked past us in the narrow streets; others sat on benches in front of their houses. A few had winter lettuce or other items for sale, but no eggs. The faces of Lang Fang's inhabitants were tanned and weather-beaten—revealing lives of hard labor and exposure to harsh conditions. The image of these terribly poor people, dressed in drab, dark blue winter clothing, and of the barren, windswept, brown landscape was depressing.

Across the track, beyond the sooty, tile-roofed, brick railroad station, we saw a group of several hundred Chinese troops bivouacked. They had stacked arms and were lounging around eating rations. Clad in mustard-colored uniforms, wrap leggings, and sneakers, they also wore the type of fatigue cap that made their ears stick straight out. We noted that their rifles were Japanese Arisakas. There were also numerous Nambu light machine guns, the kind that had given us so much misery during the war. In my limited Chinese, I asked each group of soldiers if there were any eggs for sale. Finally, a tall fellow produced a basket of fresh eggs, and we bought a dozen. Suddenly I noticed that none of these soldiers were the least bit friendly, unlike most of the other Chinese we had encountered; in fact, they were taciturn and sullen. It was unnerving that such battle-hardened veterans as my buddy and me could have been so oblivious to the mood of these troops.

Carrying our paper bag of eggs, we hurried back across the

track, only to be met by a frantic runner who told us that those were Communist troops we had been wandering among! As this was the second runner who had been sent after us, we expected to be disciplined. But our lieutenant did not notice us when we eased past him back into the compound. Soon we heard the word going around that there was a strong indication of Communist activity around the village after dark. We realized that we had already had a close call across the track.

In northern China at this time were many different armed groups—Japanese, Japanese-trained and -equipped Chinese puppet-government soldiers, Chinese Communists, Chinese Nationalists, Chinese bandits, and U.S. Marines—all armed to the teeth and vying to fill the power vacuum resulting from Japan's surrender. U.S. planes were flying Nationalist troops up to Peiping to oppose the Communists in the north. In Lang Fang and many other areas, even the surrendered Japanese were allowed to retain their arms, under U.S. supervision, in order to help fight the Communists; they were tough, highly trained, and well-disciplined troops who were best able to oppose Mao's followers until the arrival of sufficient Nationalist forces. The Chinese puppet troops were considered to be of doubtful reliability, while the bandits had no motivation to fight other than a love of plunder from the helpless farmers. The bandits sometimes called themselves Communists, but only when it seemed to be convenient; we came to believe that they would side in any fight with whomever they thought would win.

The First Marine Division's original assignment, to disarm and repatriate Japanese troops, went ahead on schedule, but as the situation became more chaotic, many of us found ourselves increasingly fighting the Communists in lonely outposts and along the railroad lines. The Communists bitterly objected to the U.S. presence and fired propaganda blasts at our high command—as well as bullets at Marines out in the boondocks. Too many Marines who had fought in World War II, and wanted to go home now that it was over, died protecting a bridge or railroad track in the wasteland of northern China.

One of the many incidents involving some of these various forces occurred at Lang Fang on 26 October, shortly after the egg quest. Breaking out our C-rations for dinner, we heated stew and coffee and boiled eggs. As the orange sun began to sink through the dust and haze, we started to shiver in the chilly evening air, even though we had sweatshirts; we had been in the Pacific so long that we were not acclimated to even the slightest cool weather. Some of us walked around inside the compound, trying to warm ourselves.

Just before sunset, a Chinese messenger arrived at the gate with a note from a puppet general seeking permission from our commanding officer to test fire a light machine gun in a sandbagged position on top of a two-story building near the railroad station. With permission apparently given, we watched several puppet soldiers working with the Nambu. To our amazement, they aimed the machine gun directly at the area where my buddy and I had been among the unfriendly troops; then they fired several long bursts. We all knew that meant trouble.

Initially, however, silence returned as darkness fell. We drifted into our quarters, wrapped ourselves in blankets, and tried to stay warm. The sentries on duty around the wall simply shivered.

Then, in less than half an hour, we heard rifle fire in the distance. The order came: "Break 'em out on the double!" Someone yelled, "Everybody outside on the double with weapons and ammo—let's move!" I pulled on my field shoes, grabbed the .45-caliber Thompson submachine gun I had carried through both Peleliu and Okinawa, rammed a twenty-round magazine in place, and tumbled outside. I headed for the fire step with everyone else. We were told to remain neutral in this fight, but if we saw anyone stick his head over the wall, we were to blow it off. The volume of rifle fire increased, and we began to hear the crash of 81mm mortar shells in the village. A Chinese ran through the dark, narrow streets tooting on a bugle. He sounded more like some drunk on New Year's Eve than any bugler I had ever heard. We were all apprehensive. Though the firing was almost unnoticeable compared to Peleliu and Okinawa, we had reason to be concerned. Here we were, about forty U.S. Marines, in the middle of what could explode into a vicious battle between two opposing Chinese forces numbering in the thousands. We had survived fierce combat in the Pacific, and now none of us wanted to stretch his luck any further and get killed in a Chinese civil war. We felt a terribly lonely sensation of being abandoned and expendable.

Then the word was passed along that Japanese troops were going out to guard the railroad station with two tanks. Most of us were not assigned to specific guard stations, so we ran the short distance to the wall bordering the road to watch this incredible scene. With our weapons slung or buttstocks resting on the fire step, we silently watched as the tanks and about thirty infantry passed by, no more than a few feet from us. Nervously, I fingered the web sling on my Thompson—the impulse to bring up the weapon to aim at our very recent enemies and squeeze the trigger was almost more than I could suppress. The Marine next to me expressed my feelings, and probably those of many of the other men, when he said, "It sure is hard not to line 'em up and squeeze 'em off."

As the lead tank slowly clanked past us, its headlights shining, we saw a Japanese officer in dress uniform and cap, Sam Browne belt, campaign ribbons, and white gloves standing erect in the turret—with his samurai saber slung over his shoulder. I wondered if I would ever understand the Japanese military. The infantrymen wore helmets and cartridge boxes, but no packs. Their Arisaka rifles were slung over their shoulders, and bayonets were fastened to their belts. The tank treads and hobnailed shoes churned up dust as they went past us and disappeared behind village buildings.

Returning to our previous positions along the wall, we learned that our CO had sent word to the Japanese major that we were neutral, but that the U.S. government would hold him responsible if any Marine was injured.

The sound of firing lasted until about midnight. Just before dawn, the Japanese came past us and returned to their barracks. At daylight, several puppet soldiers came to our gate and begged for treatment of their wounds. Our corpsman bandaged them, but he was ordered to conserve his supplies for our use. Other wounded soldiers were sent to the Japanese barracks.

The sun rose in a cloudless sky of brilliant blue. We soon heard the familiar sound of approaching Corsair engines. We watched with great satisfaction as several of the beautiful gull-winged Marine fighters flew back and forth and circled over us. The pilots waved and gave us the thumbs-up sign. The Corsairs provided a great boost to our morale as well as an impressive show of force for any watching Communists. We no longer felt isolated.

I do not remember how many days we remained in Lang Fang before another patrol relieved us, but it was not long. During this time, we were ordered to remain in or near the compound—not that any of us had the least desire to go exploring. We played baseball in a field just outside the compound gate and stayed vigilant. Fortunately, everything was quiet, and we soon returned uneventfully to Peiping.

The final G-2 report of the incident mentioned that 4,000–5,000 Communists had attacked the village, but the

Marine patrol had not been molested. There is only a brief reference to the Japanese tanks and none to the infantry with them. I have no idea whether the U.S. government really would have held the Japanese major responsible if any Americans had been injured in the skirmish. And I never learned who ordered the Japanese to send out a patrol with tanks to guard the railroad station.

The incident at Lang Fang became a bland, colorless paragraph in a routine report. But to the Marine combat veterans involved, this close call was an unforgettable experience—not so much for what happened, but for what could have happened to a small group of fugitives from the law of averages. The wheel of fortune had spun once more—and again we had survived.

Exotic Sights, Sounds, and Smells

Peiping was doubly appealing after our nerve-wracking stint in Lang Fang. A clear, sparkling cold day in October or November was a fine time for sightseeing. There was no end to the historic places to see, but my favorite place was the Forbidden City. It was located about two city blocks from the English Legation and clearly visible from the northwest section of the compound. Most public buildings were covered with green-glazed tile, but golden-glazed tile covered the buildings in the Forbidden City. The first bright, clear winter morning on which I saw the rising sun reflecting off those golden rooftops, I felt like a child again, looking at a fabled castle in a storybook. There was enough snow on the ground for contrast so that the massive walls stood out in sharp outline and the huge Throne Hall looked like it had been there forever. I saw much in China, and in Peiping particularly, to cause an American to reflect upon the brash newness of our own culture, but the Forbidden City is to China what the Parthenon is to Greece—it is the heart, soul, and symbol of China's great culture.

Frequently, several buddies and I would go to the Forbidden City and walk around the grounds and through the buildings, taking photographs and commenting on the impressiveness of it all—the way tourists are supposed to act at any famous landmark anywhere. However, my favorite times there were those when I managed to slip away from friends and wander about alone. I could marvel at it all in silent awe as I thought how ancient the place was—the massive walls, precise stone walkways and railings, and the beauty of the covered walkways and gardens. I used to sit for hours in the Throne Hall and look up at the indescribably beautiful carved ceiling—and more than once got a stiff neck in the process. Intricately carved wooden screens, columns, and frescoes held me spellbound when I contemplated the hours, or more likely years, of craftsmanship required to produce such beauty. What a blessing it had somehow escaped the destruction of war!

I had seen a picture show when I was a boy about Marco Polo and his visit to Kublai Khan in Peiping. Much of the movie had been made on a movie set depicting the Forbidden City. The Hollywood movie producers had been quite accurate, too, for I could sit out by the wall just inside the Gate of Heavenly Peace (the main entrance) and in my mind's eye see the Great Khan's men dashing about—it was like reliving the action on the genuine site and not a Hollywood set.

There was little evidence of Japanese vandalism in the Forbidden City. Exceptions were the great four-foot-high gold-plated bronze fish bowls from which most of the gold had been meticulously scraped off and carried away. The golden six-foot statue of the seated Buddha appeared unmolested and still looked down on all beholders with tranquil indifference to wars and governments. Chinese friends told me the Japanese didn't leave it intact out of benevolence but out of fear that tampering with it would inflame a massive Chinese uprising that would cause more trouble than the gold was worth—and that was saying a great deal.

The relics of ancient Chinese culture would understandably hold an American spellbound. I should say "most Americans" because, when I left Peiping after being there more than four months, I knew several men who were still making the rounds of every bar, dive, and fleshpot and had never set foot in the Forbidden City, only two blocks away.

The citizenry of Peiping was as fascinating as its ancient monuments. One of my favorite pastimes was to leave the legation and, mingling with the street traffic, walk east along Tung Chang An Chieh, past the Hotel de Pekin on the left, until I got to Hatamen Street two blocks away, where I turned left (north) and walked about three blocks to the vicinity of Tung Ssu Pai Lou. This was a large beautiful arch of wood with a tile roof that spanned the wide street. I recall that the huge wooden posts were bright red. It was very impressive. When I arrived at the arch, I would try to make myself inconspicuous to watch the crowd, leaning either against one of its posts or a tree on the side of the street. For a U.S. Marine to be inconspicuous in Peiping in 1945 was more difficult than one might suppose. In the first place our green wool uniforms marked us as victors over the Japanese—an accomplishment for which most Chinese expressed no end of gratitude, some of them even coming up to us on the street and shaking hands. Secondly, we were literally a mere handful of Caucasians in a sea of Oriental humanity. The Second and Third Battalions of the Fifth Marines plus attached units stationed in Peiping probably didn't exceed 2,500 Marines in a city of over 1.5 million Chinese. There were also the recently released Europeans from the legations who had been interned by the Japanese, but they were few in number. A Marine quietly walking down the street frequently had a group of Chinese, young and old, walking along with him—all grinning and shouting "Ding hao!" Of course there were also beggars, who trotted along begging plaintively for a hand out, "Cumshaw Joe, Cumshaw, Joe." (The number of beggars increased noticeably after it was found how generous most Marines were when a Chinese said "cumshaw.")

The stream of traffic that flowed past the arch was unlike anything I had ever seen. Automobiles were scarce, and those few I ever saw in Peiping were small, apparently of Japanese manufacture, and now used by Chinese officials. These autos were usually driven too fast with horns honking—anyone who didn't jump aside got knocked out of the way. There were a few Japanese army trucks. These were painted brown and were converted over from gasoline engines to steam. Behind the cab of each truck was an upright cylindrical boiler and furnace heated with charcoal. It was a curious sight to see a truck chugging along the street, the driver at the wheel and his assistant standing in the back of the truck tending the smoking furnace with a long iron poker or shoveling coke into the fire. Aside from the rare automobiles and more numerous Japanese steam trucks, there were our few Marine jeeps and trucks occasionally seen on the streets. A Marine infantry regiment didn't have much rolling stock.

The greatest number of vehicles one saw were rickshaws. These had a convertible top and were mounted on two wheels much like large bicycle wheels. The rickshaw coolie placed himself between the shafts of the vehicle and, holding onto these, pulled it along. These vehicles were very well balanced and lightweight and had springs beneath the seat, and brass lamps on each side. Some rickshaws were quite pretty, decorated with silver and highly polished all over. The rickshaw coolie had, in my estimation, the hardest and most strenuous job of anyone I saw in China. The typical rickshaw coolie shaved his head and wore a headband or small cap, baggy quilted cotton trousers, and quilted cotton shoes. While on the move, he usually wore only a thin shirt even in the coldest weather. When he stopped, the coolie took out his coat from a box near the passenger's footrest, put it on, and sat down on the shafts to rest. The coat was usually a moth-eaten, ragged garment of what seemed to be Angora skin with the wool turned inward. These coolies were tall and extremely thin, with their ribs often visible as though they were half starved. However, they nearly always were energetic and seemed to be good-humored. Theirs was nothing more than the existence of a beast of burden, though, and I'm sure the average farm mule in Alabama had a far easier life than a Chinese rickshaw coolie.

Some rickshaws were the tricycle type and the coolie sat on a seat and pedaled along like riding a bicycle. Curiously to me, although these rickshaws were obviously of later design and manufacture than the traditional type, they usually appeared dilapidated and in ill repair.

Conventional bicycles were a common sight but seemed to be ridden only by the more prosperous and younger people, both men and women. Collisions between bicycles and pedestrians were commonplace. In Peiping, pedestrians did not feel compelled to restrict their movement to the sidewalks, by any means. Consequently, bicycles and rickshaws frequently bumped into pedestrians, often knocking them down.

Usually no injuries resulted, but a shouting match followed each incident and invariably drew a crowd of curious bystanders. I would watch with intense amusement as a crowd formed a circle around the victims of the collision while they picked up themselves, their bicycles, and their packages and began shouting at each other. As though it had been divided evenly into two teams by someone in authority, the crowd took up the shouting and gesticulating half siding with one and half siding with the other of the accident victims. The yelling and arm flailing continued until a Chinese policeman barged in and broke it up or until fatigue caused a loss of interest in the affair. Quite frequently the crowd argued long and loud after one or both people involved in the accident had left the scene and gone about their business. I never saw any attempt on the part of anyone involved in one of these little collisions to help the other person, whether man or woman—regardless of which was at fault. Nor did the crowd offer any assistance other than shouting and arm flailing. By the same token, I never saw Chinese get so irate over these incidents that a fight resulted— arguing and gesticulating was their special way of reacting to such things that would quite likely have precipitated a fist fight in the States.

Pony carts were quite common in the stream of traffic. These were built of two heavy wooden wheels whose thick spokes were held in place on the broad wheel rim with prominent brass rivets. These carts were usually loaded with lumber, boxes, barrels, sacks of rice, or fresh winter lettuce tied on in neatly tiered rows. The coolie who drove the pony walked beside the cart, rarely riding because every inch of space was packed with freight. Sometimes this type of cart was drawn by one or two thin coolies. Each had canvas straps diagonally across his chest and leading back and attached to the cart. With a full load, the coolies had to strain and lean forward to pull the cart. They plodded along, grunting and groaning against the heavy loads, their faces drawn and pitiful from years of backbreaking labor. In China it seemed one worked hard—or starved.

The strangest carts I ever saw, and the ones I steered to the windward of, were the "honeydippers'" carts. These were pony- or mule-drawn and were much like the aforementioned carts except they had sides of tightly woven straw matting about three feet high affixed to the cart bed and held in place by wooden stakes. These carts made the rounds of the city, collecting human excrement from homes and businesses. This was then sold to farmers for use as fertilizer, or "night soil" as it was euphemistically called. On a warm day it was prudent to detour past these carts to avoid the foul odor from the semiliquid contents. Whenever I saw a full "honey" cart with its contents nearly spilling over the straw matting sides go bumping along the street, I often thought what an utter calamity it would be to collide with one of them.

The "honeydipper coolies" performed a related line of work. This type of coolie had, without a doubt, the most vile and unsavory job imaginable. He carried a deep wooden bucket slung over his back by a strap or bent loop of wood. The bucket had a wide top and tapered sharply to the bottom. The coolie carried a scoop attached to a handle. The scoops I saw were carved exactly like a human hand. The coolie plodded along the street behind mule or pony carts and camel caravans and scooped up the dung dropped by the animals. The first time I saw this type of coolie in action, it was an unforgettable experience. I stared in disbelief as the fellow went striding along, picking up the dung with the scoop held in his right hand, and with a swinging motion bringing it down into the bucket slung over his left shoulder on his back. He even had a rhythm to his motions that made it all the more amazing. Nothing was wasted in China, so as soon as the dung hit the street, the coolie scooped it up into his bucket to be sold to a farmer to fertilize his crops. Life was hard in China, and no matter how vile the task might be, it was probably the only employment that coolie could get. "What a helluva way to hafta make a livin'!" commented a buddy of mine one day as we watched a honeydipper coolie plodding along, making his collections on Chien Men Street near the Great Tower Gate where mule carts and camel caravans came through. "Yeah, that's bad duty," I answered.

Camel caravans were common in Peiping. Most of those that I saw consisted of eight to ten big, shaggy, two-humped camels and several drivers. The animals carried large loads consisting of boxes and baskets. They plodded along with an unhurried, rolling gait. I was told that they came to Peiping from the area around the Gobi Desert. The drivers were tall fellows whose facial features appeared slightly different in an indescribable way from most Chinese. I was told that most of them were Mongols, which accounted for their different features. Regardless of the finer points of their features, they were certainly a weather-beaten, hardy-looking lot of men. In cold weather they wore great long coats lined with shaggy wool, fur-lined Mongol boots with turned-up toes, and big wool-lined caps with prominent earflaps. Such clothes had been worn for centuries by men who knew how to survive the frigid winter winds of Outer Mongolia. One of the most distinctive features about the camels was their utter refusal to be hurried no matter what the driver did to them. The big animals would simply respond to any and all prodding by curling the upper lip back, stretching the neck, and making a sort of honking sound.

Peiping's pedestrians made up most of its traffic. They moved along the dusty streets in one vast flowing crowd. They reminded me of a sea of drab blue and black with yellow faces bobbing along in it, for nearly every person wore dark blue or black clothes. Regardless of the sameness of color, the crowds were fascinating to watch. I could distinguish most individuals' occupations or station in life by the type or cut of their clothes. A fat man wearing a shining black silk round hat and silk brocade blouse over long silk robes slit up the side and lined with rabbit fur would be a rich merchant. These individuals were often closely followed by their personal servant. A beautiful, pale-faced Chinese girl dressed in fine silk robes and followed by a stern-looking older woman more plainly dressed was obviously the daughter of a fine Chinese family accompanied by her servant or chaperone. On several occasions when I spoke in Chinese to such a young lady, her eagle-eyed consort stepped up beside her and spoke to her harshly in words I couldn't understand and glared at me as they both hurried along—"no acquaintance with U.S. Marine approved here" was the unspoken message, loud and clear.

Some Chinese businessmen wore certain articles of western-style clothing such as a felt hat or leather shoes, but these individuals were usually seen over on Morrison Street and in the area around the legations. Most of the more affluent men wore the Chinese-style round black silk hat with no brim and the typical Chinese-style shoes. The colder the weather, the more rabbit-fur-lined silk robes the person piled on. The poorer classes wore thickly quilted baggy cotton trousers, waist-length coats, and fur-lined hats with ear flaps. These people usually had faces that were rather tanned by exposure to the weather.

Puppet-government soldiers in mustard brown uniforms moved about quietly, not looking at all like military personnel should. Chinese Nationalists soldiers in their light blue, quilted cotton uniforms became more numerous during my time in Peiping. U.S. planes were flying them into the Peiping area in increasing numbers in the hope that they could hold the area under Chiang Kai-shek's influence and not let it fall to the Communists. The few Japanese troops I saw on the streets always saluted Marines and treated us with great respect. There were some Japanese civilians in the crowds, but now that Japan was defeated, they usually kept off the streets for fear of harm from Chinese mobs.

I saw jugglers, tinsmiths, chinaware repairmen, pedicurists, peddlers, and various other individuals who combined to make Peiping's street scenes the most fascinating one can imagine. Probably nothing as varied and as rich in individuality could be found in the western world since the London street scenes that fascinated Charles Dickens in the nineteenth century. To me, after my stay in Peiping, a street scene in the United States seemed dull and uninteresting.

All the while I stood and watched Peiping's crowds move by, there was the constant murmuring of countless conversations and the shouts of the camel drivers, peddlers, and rickshaw coolies. It all looked and sounded as though time had stood still and I was in the midst of a crowd of fascinating characters living in the eighteenth or nineteenth century. China was a timeless land. People might get in a flurry and move rapidly, or shout, "Quai, Quai (hurry, hurry)!" to a rickshaw coolie, but on the whole, daily life moved unhurriedly along just as it had for centuries. That was one of the most appealing aspects of the Peiping I saw. There was little evidence of western influence other than in the Legation Quarter, and the lack of dominance by western technology probably accounted for the rich diversity and unhurried way of life in Peiping. People were not rushing through life as victims of a timeframe set by machines, but they moved along calmly and enjoyed what pleasure and diversions their rich ancient culture afforded them, whether they were merchants or coolies.

One afternoon a buddy and I were walking down the street to a cafe for a good steak. We passed a Chinese store with much merchandise on display in the window and an imposing printed sign that read:

QUAL
ITYGO
ODS

I stopped, perplexed, and asked, "There's Chinese and there's English, but what in the world does that mean?" My friend, who had dropped out of high school to join the Marines, instantly solved the puzzle, answering, "*Quality goods,* you eight ball!" I burst out laughing. So much for my year of college.

Possibly as a result of the unhurried way of life in Peiping, the easiest thing to do there was to draw a crowd. No one, regardless of who he or she might be, was ever in too much of a rush to stop, look at, and discuss something out of the ordinary on the street.

For instance, one day a buddy and I were walking through the shopping district along Morrison Street when we saw a coolie get his cart stuck against the curb when he turned off the street up onto the sidewalk. The cart was heavily laden with lettuce, and the coolie was trying to pull it up over the curb and to a vegetable vender's stand near Tung An Market. As the poor fellow grunted and strained against the shafts and the breast band of the cart, there was a dramatic cessation in the flow of pedestrians near him. A crowd quickly formed full circle around the cart and struggling coolie. Every individual present, except the poor coolie, immediately brought each of his hands into the oversized cuffs of the opposite sleeve and began to discuss the situation in a loud voice with the next person. In no time, more people joined the circle until there must have been over a hundred people several rows deep around the cart. Everyone was babbling loudly and warming his hands while the coolie lurched and struggled against the weight of the cart—but not a single person offered to aid the straining coolie. My buddy and I got the same idea at the same instant as he said, "You take that wheel and I'll take this one, Sledgehammah." We each grabbed the spokes of one of the wheels and heaved against the weight. The cart jerked up onto the sidewalk. The surprised coolie turned around and, seeing what we had done, grinned broadly and said gratefully, "Ding hao, pungyos (very good, friends)." The crowd reacted loudly and enthusiastically to our getting the cart over the curb by each person throwing his hands into the air and shouting, "Ooh, aah, ding hao, ding hao!" and grinning, laughing, and clapping their hands. The crowd pressed around us, shaking hands with us and slapping us on the back. If the coolie tried to approach us, he couldn't because of the crowd. Finally, I said, "Let's get the hell outta here." "You can say that again," replied my buddy as we ducked the crowd and went into the large Tung An Market. "If those people thought it was so great for us to help that poor guy, why didn't they help him?" I asked in bewilderment. "Beats the hell outta me, Sledgehammah. Maybe if I was a Chinaman I could tell you," said my companion philosophically.

This same Marine came up with a routine procedure that unfailingly drew a crowd every time we pulled off the act. It was simple but always effective—I wish I had thought it up, but I must give the credit to him. One of our most successful episodes nearly got out of hand, though.

We were standing one afternoon next to the Russian Embassy on Canal Street near its intersection with Legation Street when he said, "You ready to draw a crowd?" "Righto!" I answered. He walked out into the middle of the intersection and began gazing intently at the sky directly over him. I could see him watching the pedestrians moving by him out of the corner of his eye, and when a couple of curious Chinese stopped and looked at him he began to crane his neck around still looking upward. Then he looked toward me and yelled and motioned for me to join him. I ran out to him, and he grabbed me by the shoulder and began pointing straight up into the clear blue winter sky. There was not an object to be seen, of course, but we began to talk to each other excitedly and both acted as though we were pointing out something to the other. Several curious pedestrians stopped and crowded up close, straining their eyes at the sky. They began to talk excitedly and point upward, too. My buddy and I each took a couple of Chinese men by the arm and pulled them aside a step or two and then pointed upward and said, "There it is! See it?" They of course couldn't understand what we said, but replied, "Aah, ooh, aah." Then they pointed to the sky and began showing their countrymen the correct point at which to look in the sky. A crowd rapidly gathered—all talking excitedly and pointing skyward.

We ducked out over across the street and stood on the sidewalk in front of Hotel des Wagon Lite to watch the fun. Several rickshaws got jammed in the crowd, which got larger and larger until the intersection was literally packed with people all gazing upward and talking excitedly. On all previous occasions when we had pulled off our "object in the sky" routine, the crowd would shrug their shoulders and move on shortly after we had slipped away. However, on this afternoon the press of the crowd grew worse after we slipped away from the center. People kept coming into the intersection, and those in the center began yelling to get out after a couple of rickshaws nearly tipped over. About this time we saw several Chinese policemen running west along Legation Street toward the jammed intersection. "Sledgehammah, let's shove off!" said my buddy. "Hell, yes, and on the double," I answered.

We headed east away from the crowd on Legation Street and turned left (north) onto Marco Polo Street near the French Legation. Behind us we could hear the police yelling in Chinese what I suppose was the English equivalent of "Disperse and move on." We kept running along past the French Legation until we came even with the Italian Legation, which was adjacent to the French compound. We looked back and, seeing no one following us, we slowed up to a walk. "Sledgehammah, you evah see them Chink police disperse a crowd?" "Yeah, once, and they piled into that crowd of men, women, and children swingin' billy clubs like they were knockin' dogs outta the way," I said. "Thas jus' what I mean and thas why I wanted ta get the hell outta theah," he said vehemently.

After that episode, we made it a practice to fade away from the scene before the crowd got too big. But we continued to enjoy our sky-gazing routine until we left Peiping for home. The curiosity of the people was a big factor in the success of the routine, but so was the language barrier. When the curious crowd gathered, they couldn't understand what we said and vice versa, so the pointing and feigned excitement on our part was all the more convincing to them. We never knew what the Chinese thought we, or they, saw in the sky. Peiping had been occupied by the Japanese early in the Sino-Japanese War and was never bombed at all, so its populace was spared the horror Japanese bombers had unleashed on so many Chinese cities. Now the war was over, and I don't think the crowds we drew were nervous about the possibility of hostile aircraft. I think they were just plain curious.

The weather grew increasingly colder in November and it snowed several times. The snow was very dry and powdery. We were issued long woolen underwear, heavyweight knee-length insulated parkas with hoods, and shoe-paks. The parka was made of waterproof green duck material on the outside, a great protection against snow and rain. The shoe-paks were just below-the-knee-length boots that had a rubber foot portion and leather from the shoe top up. I had owned a pair of similar hunting boots made by L. L. Bean Co. of Maine when I was a boy and knew what fine footwear they were in inclement weather. However, some of my buddies were skeptical about boots with a rubber shoe portion and a leather leg portion. It didn't take the boys long to see what fine boots these were.

FORWARD OUTPOST

During late November or early December, K Company was sent out to Lantienchang Airfield, nine miles northwest of Peiping, to pull a week-long tour of guard duty. The weather was bitterly cold. The north wind swept down out of Mongolia like an icy blast. There wasn't much snow and what was there was so powdery that it blew away, uncovering the ubiquitous North China dust. We wore long underwear, green wool trousers, and our winter gear we had just been issued. We didn't take the mortars because our detail was to stand guard duty on posts around the hangars and buildings and not be deployed in combat formation.

The Japanese had used Lantienchang Airfield, or North West Airfield as it was called, and I imagine had constructed many buildings there. We were billeted in a two-story Japanese barracks. The heating system had been torn out, apparently by the Japanese when the war ended, and the building was like an icebox. It was a well-constructed masonry building, but the most one could say for it during our stay was that it shielded us from the icy wind—for that, at least, we were thankful. The building was divided into rooms big enough for four men each, so we assumed it had been officers' quarters, perhaps for pilots.

Three buddies and I were assigned a room that was typical. It was devoid of furniture, but the entire floor was covered with thick, smoothly woven straw mats like those we had seen in some Okinawan houses during the campaign there. Our bedrolls had been left in the legation, so we slept in all our clothes and wrapped in our blankets to try to stay warm. This sort of thing in itself was not considered a hardship by combat veterans. However, there were Army Air Corps and Marine Air Wing people stationed in adjacent buildings that were heated and warm, and we bitterly resented that. Peiping's comforts had spoiled us.

Our chow, heated C-rations, was served in an unheated tent on wooden tables. After eating in Peiping's fine restaurants, we had little appetite for C-rations served out into our mess gear in a frigid tent. Combat-infantry veterans being accomplished scroungers, we soon located a fine, heated galley in a wooden building where army and Marine air people were fed. Because different aircrews came and went on the airfield, some of us managed to eat several meals undetected in the cozy galley, where tables were set with clean white cloths and food served on plates. Finally, one day, a man on mess duty came over to four of us seated at a table drinking hot joe and said, "You guys from the rifle company on guard out here?" "Yeah, and what of it?" replied one of my buddies in a belligerent manner. "Oh, I just wondered," said the mess man. We thought for sure this would be the end of our scrounging hot joe and meals at the galley, but no one said anymore to us, and we only went over for one meal a day after that.

Whenever someone from K Company went into Peiping on liberty, he returned ladened with packages of food we had him buy for us—we avoided those C-rations by every means we could. They were combat rations, and they'd served us well under those conditions, but the damned war was over and this was occupation duty—and we had a right to a hearty appetite!

During the period K Company was on guard detail at Lantienchang, we stood what was called "interior guard duty." There was little "interior" about it, except it was the type of guard duty procedure followed in established camps and on military bases. We were "on 4 and off 8" hours, with every third day off duty. A K Company officer was OD (officer of the day); there was a sergeant of the guard, a corporal of the guard, and then the members of the guard detail. We were assigned posts at various places around the buildings and outskirts of the airfield, which was surrounded by a simple barbed-wire fence. The OD and/or the sergeant of the guard came around periodically, unannounced, and inspected us. We didn't walk a formal route on our guard posts but were ordered to move about environs; we could stop but not sit down. Orders were to report any unauthorized personnel (non–U.S. military) in the area to the corporal of the guard. We carried loaded weapons (I carried my father's .45) on duty. Orders were not to fire our weapons unless absolutely necessary. If anyone didn't respond to orders to halt or leave the area immediately, we were to call the corporal of the guard. If we were at all suspicious of danger or threatened, we were to shoot to kill. All the men were combat veterans, and many recently recovered from wounds received on Okinawa (our first replacements hadn't come into China yet). They were well versed in the doctrine of fire discipline—but wouldn't have hesitated to shoot down anything or anybody they considered a threat. The Chinese from the little village outside the airfield must have known this. They were as friendly as Peiping's citizens when I went sightseeing in their village, but they avoided the airfield completely except when on authorized work details.

As luck would have it, I was assigned the afternoon watch

(1200 to 1600 hours) and the midwatch (2400 to 0400). I guarded an interesting post. It was a Japanese aircraft hangar housing several Zero fighter planes that had been undergoing repairs and maintenance when the Japanese left. Outside, just off the concrete apron, Zeros and two-engine bombers were parked.

Either the Japanese, before they left, or the local Chinese before we arrived, had stripped the hangar of all portable tools and the planes of most instruments. Still, it was a fascinating place. Some of my buddies were posted out on the edge of the field along the barbed-wire fence with the dusty, brown airfield on one side, stubbled fields across the fence, and the arid, brown mountains in the distance. Except for the poor little village near the airfield gate, the place was surrounded by barren, desolate landscape.

During the midwatch, all of us on the guard walked briskly around our posts, stamped our feet, and swung our arms as the icy wind whistled across the airfield out of Mongolia to the north. (I shudder to think what the wind-chill factor must have been.) Each of us wore every item of winter clothing issued us, including hooded parkas and shoe-pak boots. But those of us with years in the tropics weren't acclimated to such bitterly cold weather. The OD allowed each guard to build a fire from scrap wood. One still had to patrol one's post but at least could warm up periodically. This greatly reduced our misery, particularly during the midwatch. During the afternoon watch, the usually cloudy weather wasn't as severely cold because there wasn't much wind.

The first day the cold weather was crystal clear. The afternoon watch fell out about 1130 to be posted to our various guard posts. The OD inspected us. Every aspect of our uniforms, weapons, and gear being acceptable to his eagle eye, he ordered the corporal of the guard to "post the guards." The

Marine I relieved at my post reported all well. I walked around to familiarize myself with the area. The corporal marched his detail off to the next post. The sound of their rubber soled shoe-paks clumping on the concrete was unlike that of our familiar boondockers.

An occasional U.S. C-47 transport plane landed at the field. Each taxied on past the hangar where I was to the nearby area used by U.S. Army and Marine units. Consequently, I never saw who got off those planes. We were told the pilots were flying in blue-uniformed troops of Chiang's Nationalist Army. They would protect Peiping from the Communists. A lean, jovial Chinese lieutenant of the puppet-government army was busy directing a working party of coolies in cleaning up the area. He appeared as snug and warm in his brown, cotton-padded uniform as I was in my bulky parka, green wool trousers, and "longhandles" (woolen underwear). The coolies wore ragged, faded blue or black padded cotton clothing. They were thin and showed every evidence of living in the utmost poverty. But they were as energetic as the lieutenant in their work. They were probably thankful to have employment during the frigid winter months while their fields lay fallow.

The lieutenant introduced himself to me. I wish I remembered his name—he was a friendly man. He was pleased to the point of jubilation to find that I was interested in and understood a little of his language. (Hao's teaching me Chinese was already proving valuable.) Upon discovering my interest in his language, the lieutenant talked to me increasingly during the first couple of days he had his working party around the hangar. I really understood little of what he said, although he spoke the same dialect (Mandarin) as Hao. He told me the story of his life in daily installments. And he was sincerely interested in hearing mine.

I did my best—but my knowledge of his language was simply so minute compared to what that officer had convinced himself it to be that I realized I had a real problem. What had begun with the exchange of a few Chinese words and phrases now evolved into utterly incomprehensible lengthy monologues by the lieutenant, these interrupted periodically by his shouts to his coolies. Also, to my despair, he frequently exhibited animated quizzical expressions on his face coupled with a question asking my opinion on some subject or other. I was "in deep water." This began to exhaust me. It also began to bear uncomfortable similarity to those grim recitations in second-year high school Latin under the demanding tutelage of dear old Miss Edith Duffie. I recall I had agreed with a fellow sufferer in that class that it was amazing how the Romans had built a vast empire—and had time to learn Latin. Now, I couldn't understand how the Chinese had built the Great Wall, the Forbidden City, and other marvels as well as learning Chinese—to say nothing of writing the complex characters.

The unexpected appearance of Hao solved my dilemma. The company houseboys were brought out in a Marine truck to do certain tasks for the company guard detail. When I didn't have the duty, and Hao wasn't working, I took him aside and explained my problem in my pidgin Chinese and in English. He sized it up in a jiffy. We went immediately to the hangar, found my officer "pungyo (friend)," and engaged him in an hour-long conversation. The lieutenant first looked askance at Hao when he realized he was a servant. However, when I told him Hao and I were "ding hao pungyos," all class distinction evaporated on his part.

Later that afternoon, Hao brewed us each a cup of that delicious aromatic jasmine tea I learned to love so well on a frigid North China evening, a tea that warmed the soul as well as the body. As we sat on the floor mats, he told me about the lieutenant. The son of a farmer, the man had joined the puppet army, not out of loyalty to the Japanese, but due to wartime economic conditions. He rose through the ranks and hoped to join Chiang's army when the Nationalists took over North China.

From then on when I encountered the lieutenant, things went well. I simply used what little Chinese I knew plus some new phrases Hao taught me and said "ding hao" or "boo hao" at what appeared the appropriate points in the conversation. When neither of these was called for, I tried to look philosophical and gravely exclaimed, "Ooh! Aah!" or "Umh, ahh." Fortunately, the officer "talked" a great deal with his hands and facial expressions. This, of course, helped my comprehension. Our conversations, or his monologues, continued during the entire week at the airfield. The lieutenant and I parted great friends— he apparently having convinced himself his "Maline pungyo" spoke fluent Chinese.

Marine and army personnel came by my post periodically and stopped to "shoot the breeze" or exchange the latest scuttlebutt. They were maintenance personnel for the U.S. planes on the field. Most told me they had recently come overseas, many of them en route to the Philippines when the war ended. Most of the Marine air personnel were openly apologetic about not having participated in active combat during the war. I always responded with, "What you were spared greatly exceeded what you missed." Also, we had all been ordered to our certain duties by the high command.

In interesting contrast, most army personnel were rather frank in stating that they had sought maintenance and quartermaster jobs to avoid combat. Their selfish attitude, lack of any feeling of responsibility to the war effort, or even any patriotism I found disgusting. Thinking of the suffering of our casualties, I replied to these with certain well-chosen remarks to shame them and sting what conscience they might have had—if any. When I explained the "George Medal" attitude (when the stuff hits the fan let George do it) to them, they usually had somewhere they needed to get on to in a hurry. These people seemed to regard infantrymen as a rather wild, reckless breed, not because of anything we said or did around them, but because of what little they understood of our combat experiences.

The aircrews, both Marine and army, were completely at ease around us. They respected the hazards we had endured because they had encountered great risks themselves in their line of duty. Our respect was mutual. They found it difficult to comprehend how we had endured the perils, horrors, and hardship of infantry combat. We found it difficult to understand the cool nerve required of a man who takes his chances in a flimsy aircraft—in or out of combat.

On a couple of occasions, I did express a hostile attitude to some of the maintenance personnel. One man asked me if I knew of any Chinese who would buy a Thompson submachine gun. This character came ambling by my post one day and, having seen me talking to the Chinese lieutenant earlier, asked me confidentially if I thought the officer would like to buy a Tommy gun. "What the hell are you talking about?" I said. "Well, I got to the Philippines just after the war ended and was stationed at an airbase in Zamboanga. One day I took a Thompson from the warehouse, field stripped it, and stowed the parts in my sea bag. I've been told these Chinks'll pay $200 for a Thompson," he answered. "Hell, that lieutenant probably don't make $5.00 a month. How's he gonna buy a $200 weapon?" I replied. "Oh, I don't mean sell it to *him*, maybe his government will buy it. If they won't, how can I contact the Communists? I don't care which side buys it—boy what I could do with $200!" he said excitedly. I blew my stack! "Are you Asiatic? If you sell that Tommy to the Communists and they attack this airfield who the hell you think they're gonna shoot with it?—my buddies and me, that's who," I said hot with anger. "Oh, hell," he said calmly, "200 bucks is 200 bucks, and I've been lugging that Tommy around a long time. I'm afraid I might get caught with it."

This man's utterly callous attitude toward the possible use of the weapon against us was beyond belief. He saw I was mad as hell so he shoved off. I reported the conversation to the OD He said an investigation would be made right away, even if it required a shake-down inspection of the man's unit. The lieutenant was as mad about it as I was. I never heard any more of the incident and never found out whether the money-grubbing thief got caught or not. Many of us had made "moonlight requisitions" during the war; however, usually it was chow or uniforms and socks for our own use. On rare occasions when we stole automatic weapons from rear-area troops, it was to give us more firepower against the Japanese—never to sell to an enemy who might use it against our own men!

I have always regretted that I didn't pull my .45 on that character, call the corporal of the guard to put the man under arrest, and search his sea bag. However, he might have been just boasting about possessing the Tommy—I had no evidence but his talk.

The first night on my post, the guard I relieved had already built a cheerful fire in front of the hangar and had plenty of wood piled nearby. While the clomping sound of the guard detail's shoe-paks died away as they marched on through the frigid darkness, I drew closer to the bright fire. It cast flickering shadows onto the front of the hangar and the Japanese planes parked nearby. Although no wind was blowing, the intense cold made the fire a luxury.

What a helluva place to be on a night like this, I thought, as I lit my pipe. Those rear-echelon people over there in heated buildings, and the infantrymen roughing it as usual. However, it could be worse, I mused. The war was over. We would return to Peiping soon. Anyway, it wouldn't be so long before I was sent home on the point system based on time overseas and number of campaigns. I might as well see and enjoy some of the fascinating aspects of China before leaving. So I began to think, not of home, but of how I planned to go over every inch of the Forbidden City as soon as we returned to Peiping. Actually, of all the places to be sent on occupation duty in Asia, we had lucked into the best of them all. Then I began to feel like a fortunate tourist in one of the world's most unique areas, not a lonely, shivering, homesick veteran of two of the war's bloodiest campaigns. The fire was cheery, the dancing shadows were pretty, I felt warm inside, *and* the war *was* over.

Nevertheless, I couldn't suppress my instinctive urge to periodically look behind me and to loosen the flap on my .45 pistol holster. (The critical necessity of keeping watch for Japanese infiltrators during many long nights on Peleliu and Okinawa had developed an instinct that would require years to overcome.) But otherwise, guard duty didn't seem so bad after all.

Suddenly, the old terror gripped my entire being in its soul-crushing grasp. My ears, though not consciously listening, had picked up that most dreaded of all sounds—artillery shells passing overhead! I went into a crouching position, my heart pounded, my throat tightened, my mouth went dry, my stomach churned, my whole body went rigid. Oh, God, please, no! I prayed. But my combat-fine-tuned ears picked up the vibrations, sent them to my terror-stricken brain, which—through experience—clicked off the information to my consciousness like some automatic electronic device. Rustling sounds of shells passing over high, not "whistling" or "whining," that's good: won't strike near here; 75mm guns, three or four of them, firing in battery: guns a long distance from my position—thus came the "message" as though sent by telegraph. (Ears that had aided me in being among K/3/5's 35 percent unwounded survivors of Peleliu and less than 1 percent on Okinawa could be trusted.)

After what seemed an eternity, there came the "bum, bum, bum, bum" of the exploding shells far away in the hills, closely followed by the faint thudding of the reports of the guns far away in the other direction. I reported this to the corporal of the guard, who came along making his rounds about then. He was amazed—and left to check it out. He came by a few minutes later and said, "Sledgehammer, the OD checked with Regiment in Peiping about them shells passing over here. The scoop is that it's Chinese Nationalists firing long-range over this area at Communist positions in them mountains. He said the Nationalists know we are here and they'll keep an eye on their range so as we don't get any short rounds." "Good-oh," I replied, "but it still gives me the shakes hearin' the damn things goin' over." "Me, too, it's like bein' on Okinawa all over again and wonderin' when a short round'll knock ya to hell and back. I wish them Chinks would do their shellin' at each other when we ain't in between 'em," he said.

The next night a salvo of shells passed over at exactly the same time. Thereafter, each night I arranged my patrolling in the vicinity of my post so that I was always in the hangar at the time the packages of terror and death went whistling overhead. This solved the problem of my jitters caused by that most dreaded of sounds to a combat veteran. The Nationalists always fired their artillery at exactly the same time each night, so I arranged to be standing at that exact time well inside the silent, dark, frigid hangar among the parked Zeros—ghosts of a once proud and powerful air force. The corporal agreed with me that we had heard enough shells—no matter how far away. "If that's supposed to be harassing fire against the Communists, how the hell the Nationalists think it's effective fire if they let go at the exact same time every night? All the Communists gotta do is get in their dugouts, just like you go in that hangar, and wait 'til that artillery fire comes in, kicks up a lotta dust, and don't hurt nobody. Then they can come out of their shelters. I can't figure how these people fight a war," he said, scratching his head. "Me, neither," I said, "but if it was Nips firing those guns, they would set their timing so and catch the Communists by surprise and blow 'em sky high." "You can say that again," answered the corporal.

One dark night, with a frigid, blustery wind sweeping down out of the northern hills, I stood with my back to the crackling fire and thought this was about the coldest weather I had ever experienced. The fire cast its dancing glow and resulting flickering shadows over most of the area in front of the hangar. It was easy to understand why primitive man had greatly cherished his campfire, I thought. It not only warmed and cheered me, but it also pushed back the blackness of night, where danger might be lurking.

But for me, there were no dangers in the shadows—the war was over. Also, it was very unlikely the Communists would risk causing us any trouble, for they had their hands full at this time in the civil war with the Nationalists and had no desire to tangle with U.S. military power in North China.

As I slowly turned around, following the habit of periodically scanning the darkness all around me, I turned and faced the fire. It was about time for a pipe, I thought, as I reached for my tobacco pouch and pipe in the side pocket of my parka. The instant I faced the fire, I saw I was not alone out there! In one rapid reflex, learned in training and perfected in combat, I snatched my big .45 from its holster with my right hand, jerked the slide rearward with my left, and released it so it snapped forward and threw a round into the chamber as I brought the pistol up to firing position. There in the full light of the fire, and not more than fifteen feet from me, was a tremendous dog, a black German Shepherd. He began snarling with a deep-throated growl. His huge white fangs were gleaming in the firelight as he slowly inched toward me on his belly. The dog had obviously been preparing to spring onto my back just as I had happened to turn around. I leveled the .45 at his head and sighted it between his large yellow eyes—fierce, slanted eyes more like those of a wolf than a dog. He was very large, certainly weighing well over a hundred pounds—all of which seemed to be muscle. I took up the trigger slack as I aimed between his eyes. He stopped creeping toward me as our eyes met.

We stared at each other. The big dog hesitated because he had lost the element of surprise. There was no doubt as to his intentions, but I wasn't afraid. As I started to squeeze the trigger and send the big bullet crashing into his skull, I hesitated. Suddenly, I was overcome with the realization that this was the most magnificent, beautiful dog I had ever seen. Being a sentimental dog lover, I could not bear to squeeze the trigger—even under these precarious circumstances. I had never killed a dog and was shocked at the idea I might have to kill such a superb animal—stalking me though he was. What irony, what a paradox, I thought. No more than a few months before I had shot men, Japanese soldiers, during the Okinawa campaign and prior to that on Peleliu—shot and killed members of the human race without the slightest hesitation or remorse. That was war, and they were trying to kill me. Now this huge, snarling, vicious dog was almost at the point of springing on me from behind just as I turned around—but I couldn't shoot him. How strange it was, I thought, that I had killed men who were a threat to me, but it was unthinkable to kill this splendid dog—who was also a threat to me.

For a brief period I stared through the sights of my pistol into those piercing yellow eyes. He returned my gaze. His fierce burning eyes were riveted on mine. They were like none I had ever seen. Finally, he blinked and glanced away—an indication among canines that resolve is fading. He slowly rose up on all fours and gracefully trotted off into the shadows (he appeared to glide along) and out of sight behind the hangar. Only then did the realization come to me that he could stalk one of my buddies, who might not be as lucky as I had been in discovering the big beast before it sprang. So I called the corporal of the guard and reported the incident.

Next day I was told that the big dog I had seen was a real threat. Apparently, he was one of several trained guard dogs the Japanese had used in patrolling the area around the airfield. The Chinese in the village vowed the dogs were extremely vicious and had been released and left behind just to cause as much trouble as they could after the Japanese evacuated Lantienchang.

Scuttlebutt among the K Company Marines was that the OD said a detail would be formed to seek out and shoot the Japanese guard dogs. I never knew whether this was true or not—but, in any event, I did not want to be on any detail to shoot such fine dogs, no matter how vicious.

The next night I had duty the dog problem became more serious. After making my rounds on my post in and around the hangar, I heaped wood on the fire and stamped my shoe-paks on the concrete to warm myself. Old Man Winter was roaring out of the northern hills with a vengeance. All was quiet except for the voice of the icy wind, which was blowing dust and wisps of dry snow around the hangar. No one but the guard detail was out in that frigid wind sweeping across the airfield. I was keeping an eye on my wristwatch so I could make a turn into the hangar at the time the nightly salvo of Nationalist Chinese artillery shells passed overhead. Looking forward to *not* hearing that event became habit.

Suddenly, I heard the thudding of running feet between the hangar and the adjacent building. Who in the world could that be, I wondered, as I started to investigate. A terrified, desperate voice began screaming in Chinese. I could not understand the words, but whatever they were, they signaled, "Help!" The screams made cold chills chase each other up and down my spine. They reminded me of those horrifying sounds accompanying the desperate hand-to-hand fight with the Japanese that so often occurred on the front lines at night.

I raced across the concrete apron in front of the hangar, drawing and chambering a round in my .45 as I ran. Holding the big pistol "at the ready," muzzle upward and the thumb safety switched on, I rounded the front corner of the hangar at a dead run. In the dim firelight I saw a young Chinese man running toward me. He was yelling for help and had an expression of consummate terror on his face. I immediately recognized him as one of the civilian workers in the Army Air Corps mess hall. At that instant, he was no more than twenty feet in front of me. He pitched forward headlong onto the deck. As he went down, he appeared to be jerked off his feet. He saw me and yelled, "Ooh, pungyo (oh, friend)!"

I stopped instantly. As I did, I saw a huge dog, possibly the same one that had stalked me previously. Its big jaws were clasped firmly around one of the man's ankles. It uttered not a sound. As surprised to see me as I was to see him, the dog released the man. I flipped off the thumb safety and brought the .45 down, aiming between the dog's eyes. It responded with a growl and bared its fangs. With the man flat on the ground between my target and me I hesitated before firing—a reflex born of countless lectures on fire discipline and firearms safety. It was fortunate that I paused, because the man tried to jump up at that moment. Had I fired, I would have hit him for certain.

The dog spun around and ran silently off in the shadows behind the hangar. I holstered my pistol and ran to the injured man. As I tried to look at the injury to his ankle, he kept trying to get up on his hands and knees and run. Finally, I pushed him back down on his belly and took a look at his ankle in the dim light. The thick, quilted cotton trousers bound at the ankle with a cloth band had afforded considerable protection against the dog's teeth. However, the big fangs had made several puncture wounds, and there was bleeding. I tried to tell the man I would call a corpsman and to remain still. The poor fellow was so terrified, as I would have been had I been in his place, that he insisted on getting up. This he did, bowed, shook hands with me, and took off for the nearby village as fast as he could limp along.

I reported the episode to the corporal of the guard. The OD said he would see to it that the Chinese man was given a tetanus shot on the morrow.

After that encounter—which certainly confirmed the ferocity of those dogs—I saw no more of them. Likewise, the Chinese victim of the attack never again took the shortcut passing the hangar to his village. He thanked me profusely for my help. Next time I slipped into the chow hall where he worked, he showed his gratitude by bringing me so much extra food I was afraid the mess sergeant might take notice.

CROWD CONTROL

One night Paul Wachendorfer, a buddy of mine and an Okinawa veteran, returned from liberty in Peiping with exciting news that was to have tremendous influence on both of us during the ensuing months we were in the capital. He had had the good fortune to meet a very nice English-speaking Chinese family as the result of a rather unique sequence of events.

Paul had gone into the city that afternoon on the USMC liberty truck that took us to and from Peiping. It was a beautiful, clear, cold day, and as he was walking down Morrison Street in the Legation Quarter, trying to warm up after the windy ride in the open truck, he noticed a crowd of Chinese gathering.

Now, as I mentioned earlier, it didn't take much to draw a crowd on the streets of Peiping in 1945. Each gathering evolved through a series of definite stages as predictable as the phases of the moon—but fleeting in nature. The embryogenesis and ultimate fading away of a crowd of Peiping's citizens was a well-known phenomenon to any "China Hand." It was as fascinating as it was predictable. First, one or two pedestrians stopped to observe some event—even though it might be only slightly out of the ordinary. Soon other pedestrians or cyclists stopped and asked the first onlookers what was transpiring. A detailed explanation was always given in reply. On such occasions the Chinese exhibited not the slightest reticence to converse freely with any and all strangers. Immediate rapport was established between the initial observers and the curious newcomers. Each then bent his arms at the elbows and placed each hand inside the cuff of the opposite sleeve to warm them. Then a lively discussion of the observed situation ensued. As other people came up, the process was repeated. In proportion to the increase in the size of the crowd, it also become necessary for each conversation to become louder in order to be heard over the many voices of other spectators. The larger the crowd grew, the more rapidly newcomers ran up and joined in, like the gravitational pull of some large celestial body attracting smaller individual particles—the bigger it was, the stronger the pull and the faster the accretion.

Newcomers had to crane their necks, stand on tiptoes, or jump up and down to see over the heads and shoulders of spectators in front of them. The mood of the crowd depended on the nature of the observed event. I have seen crowds of over a hundred people gather around a rickshaw with a flat tire or a cart with a broken wheel. Animated conversation was the general attitude until, finally, interest waned and the crowd dispersed, each member quietly going his own way.

When the center of attraction was anything of a controversial nature, such as a bicycle collision or an argument between a street vendor and a customer, the crowd behaved accordingly. Half the crowd invariably took the side of one of the aggrieved persons, and the other half supported the opponent. Loud shouting and much arm waving and gesticulating always accompanied these events. The crowd dispersed when wearied by the argument. Usually, though, this type of crowd was dispersed by one or more sharp-eyed policemen.

Peiping's policemen wore black uniforms, barracks hats with silver badges, military-cut tunics, trousers, wrap leggings, and rubber-soled canvas shoes. A Sam Browne belt held a billy club and a wooden-holstered German Mauser machine pistol, which extended from the waist to knee. Every policeman I ever saw was about five feet, seven inches tall, thin as a rail, and probably didn't weigh an ounce over about 110 pounds. Like Japanese soldiers, their size belied their determination to do their job.

Policemen seemed to gauge their mood by that of the crowd

rather than vice versa. If the crowd was calm, I've seen Peiping's policemen quietly walk among them and tell them to disperse—which they usually did without delay. If the crowd was boisterous, a single policemen would wade into a mob of packed humanity yelling and screaming orders. He would swing his club right and left with such indiscriminate abandon that he sent men, women, and children scurrying in every direction, holding the aching bumps and bruises on heads and shoulders. The policeman's excitement would not abate until the crowd was dispersed. His authority never seemed to be questioned—possibly because of the ominous threat implied in the huge Mauser holster swinging from the skinny waist.

If such behavior appeared to an American as an excessive use of force, it must be remembered that China had been a war-torn country for years. Although fortunately never a battle-ground, Peiping was occupied by large numbers of Japanese troops. Any crowd not readily dispersed by Chinese civilian police would surely have brought Japanese troops to the scene. The emperor's troops had demonstrated in numerous cities their unhesitating and reckless use of the bayonet on any and all Chinese who did not follow orders immediately. Any form of resistance to the invaders invariably precipitated such ruthless brutality against innocent civilians as that at Nanking, beyond the imagination and belief of most Americans snug and safe in the States. The Japanese considered the Chinese, and others of their enemies, to be inferior. Therefore, resistance was not only to be overcome swiftly but also punished with incredible brutality (a page of history that is already being glossed over now, barely fifty years later). But those of us who had fought the Japanese on the front lines of Peleliu, Okinawa, and other Pacific battles understood the propensity for cruelty on the part of Japanese troops far better than journalists, diplomats, or historians. So the bumps and bruises administered by Peiping police were understandably preferable to, and a safeguard against, the bayonets of the cruel invaders.

The crowd Paul happened on that day was already pretty riled up when he came along. Being rather tall, he easily looked over the people and spotted the focus of all the disturbance. A panic-stricken rickshaw coolie was desperately trying to prevent his vehicle from being tipped over by the angry crowd. His passenger, clinging precariously to the seat, rocking to and fro, was a pretty but very frightened young Japanese woman. She was stylishly and beautifully dressed in a gray wool suit of the latest American fashion—it appeared to be right out of *Vogue*. Powerful and barrel-chested, Paul pushed his way through the crowd as though he were wading through tall grass. Shouting chivalric imprecations against anyone who would attack a helpless woman—Japanese or otherwise—he grabbed the woman by one elbow, stuffed some money in the rickshaw coolie's trembling hands, and waded through the other side of the crowd.

On seeing a U.S. Marine grab her, the woman at first thought her executioner, or worse, was at hand. Fortunately, she spoke English and soon realized Paul was her salvation from a dangerous situation. He hurried her along the street and, looking back as they rounded a corner, saw they were not being followed, the crowd probably thinking he was carrying her off to a fate worse than they could deliver up.

Paul hailed a couple of rickshaws and told the woman he would see her home safely. Assuming his intentions were honorable, or that he was her only hope, she thanked him profusely and told him where she lived. Paul escorted her to a small house on one of Peiping's narrow labyrinthine *hutungs* (streets). There, Miss Morita, as the woman had introduced herself, lived with her elderly mother. The latter, upon answering a knock at the door, all but fainted at the sight of a U.S. Marine standing behind her pretty daughter—thinking this must certainly be retribution for the attack on Pearl Harbor, she later said. However, Miss Morita quickly recounted the recent events in Japanese to her parent, who didn't know English. The old lady was all smiles, and Paul was invited in for a cup of tea.

After many expressions of gratitude from mother and daughter for saving Miss Morita from the angry crowd, Paul said he must leave. He was invited to come again for tea. He then returned to the area where he had encountered the crowd, but all was quiet. Seething with angry resolve, Paul hurried along to demand of the first English-speaking Chinese he could find why anyone would be so filled with hatred as to threaten an obviously innocent young woman, even if she was Japanese.

It was Paul's good fortune—and especially mine—that he encountered a striking-looking Catholic priest who had not only witnessed the incident but could also speak fluent English, Chinese, Russian, French, Japanese, and his native Flemish. He was Fr. Marcel von Hemelryjck from Belgium, a former prisoner of the Japanese, and he answered Paul's rather heated question about the Chinese crowd's behavior by stating mildly: "What they did was not right, and it is fortunate you saved her, my son. But the Chinese cannot so soon forget these years of brutal treatment by the Japanese—and she *was* Japanese."

The clear logic of his answer caused Paul to understand the realities of life in postwar China and the obvious necessity to repatriate all Japanese to their home islands as soon as possible. He had a cup of coffee with Father Marcel at a nearby cafe. Father Marcel invited Paul to accompany him to the home of a Chinese family he knew. Paul went, met them, and found them to be delightful people. After a nice conversation he asked if he could bring a friend to visit them, and they insisted he do so.

Paul rushed back from liberty that cold night into the frigid squad room almost too excited to talk. He asked me to go with him to visit the Soongs next liberty. "Sledgehammer, you've got to meet these people as soon as we get back to Peiping. God, they are nice people, and Father Marcel is a great guy. I visited with this Chinese family he took me to see, and we had the finest food I've had in China." Thus, I was soon to enter into one of the most rewarding and pleasant episodes of my life— my friendships with Father Marcel and Dr. Y. K. Soong and family.

That night Paul and I both had guard duty. So in the miserable cold of our unheated little room in the old Japanese barracks, we donned every item of winter clothing we had, got our mess kits, and went to chow. We headed over to the K Company galley—an unheated tent erected in a stubbled field nearby. The clank and rattle of our mess kits was barely audible above the howling of the icy wind. As Paul talked animatedly of the Soong family, I looked over toward the Army Air Corps chow hall. Cheerful bright lights streamed out the clean glass windows. Inside I could see white-clad mess men (KPs, as the army called them) setting tables covered with white cloths. As Paul and I entered the cold galley tent, dimly lit by a lamp, and crowded with our K Company buddies bundled up as we were against the biting cold, I thought of the popular World War II saying back in the States about America's fighting men: "Nothing is too good for our troops." And as a buddy back on Pavuvu had added sardonically, "Consequently the troops get nothing."

Even now, after the war, the amenities of life seemed to be made available only to noncombatants and rear-echelon troops. But the public never seemed to realize this. So Paul and I stood at a table of roughhewn boards and ate corned-beef hash from our mess kits.

BACK TO ENGUA FOO

After our guard duty assignment on the airfield, we boarded open trucks for the bumpy ride back to our billets in Engua Foo. The bumpy road was the least of our discomforts. The weather had turned bitterly cold, and we shivered on the windy open trucks until our teeth chattered, even though we were wearing all the clothes we could pile on. However, closed trucks would have been more appropriate for rear-echelon troops— Marine infantry weren't supposed to notice such minor inconveniences as being chilled to the bone in an open truck on a winter day in North China.

About an inch of snow blanketed Peiping. I had never seen much snow and was amazed how certain terrain and structural features were accentuated by the clean white covering over everything. However, in the streets it was already turning into dirty brown slush mixed with camel and horse dung.

Upon returning to the legation, we went to our squad bays, stored our weapons and gear, grabbed up our mess kits, and headed for evening chow. The chow, I remember vividly, was hot joe (which warmed us), stringy bully beef (which revolted us), dehydrated mashed potatoes (with an aftertaste like tin cans), and fresh fruit. The latter we relished. Most of the rest I emptied into a can held by a Chinese worker outside the building. He grinned and thanked me sincerely. I asked him if he would feed it to his hogs—he said no, he'd give it to his grateful family. Such was the severe poverty in China. I always heaped-up my mess kit with food I didn't intend to eat in order to give it to that man.

When I had entered the mess halls, I had noticed the snow on the several stone steps and the landing had been packed into ice by Marine boondockers. So when I came out of the hall, I walked gingerly down the steps. Unfortunately, some of my buddies hadn't noted the ice. They came rushing out of the mess hall headed to the slop chute for a beer. When the first five or six rushed out onto the landing, their feet flew out from under them, and with rattling mess kits, they flew through the air and sprawled onto the frozen ground in a heap. Roars of laughter met them from more careful Marines already outside. The fallen got up, cursed, and joined the laughter as each new unfortunate came sailing through the air.

Several days after our return, about forty of us were detailed for an honor guard meeting a U.S. Army general arriving at Nan Yuan Airfield about eight miles south of Peiping. We wore dungarees and combat gear. We were trucked to the site in vehicles with their tarps battened down against the weather. Fortunately, it was a clear balmy day, but we wore sweatshirts under our dungarees. We formed up in platoon formation, opened ranks, and stood inspection by the general (and several Marine officers). He wore an army dress uniform and many campaign ribbons and was a distinguished-looking man. Because of my height, I was near the rear of the second squad. The general, whose name I do not recall, inspected us with meticulous care and an eagle eye. As he passed near me I heard him ask the Marine captain in charge where we had fought. The captain told him, and the general remarked, "This is the finest looking group of troops I've ever seen." A kind comment from a brother service.

The Soong Family

Meeting the Soong family and Father Marcel was one of the happiest events of my entire life. The first liberty I had back at Engua Foo, my buddy Paul Wachendorfer and I hailed a couple of rickshaws outside the legation gate, and he gave them the Soongs's address. Both coolies grunted in a knowing way, but I asked them in Chinese if they knew where we wanted to go. They both nodded in the affirmative, and one said in broken English, "Oh, ah, you Maline wanta pretty Chinese girs." "Hell no!" yelled my buddy, and I yelled "Boo hao (no good)!" in Chinese as they turned their vehicles and trotted for the main street. "Pretty Chinese girs," both coolies repeated. Realizing we would undoubtedly end up in front of some Chinese bawdy house instead of our destination, I jumped out of my rickshaw and trotted beside my coolie. I grabbed his collar and pulled him to a halt. I stuck my face in his face, despite his garlic breath, and spoke to him in Chinese. He looked puzzled but repeated what I said. His face broke into a broad grin (which would have given a dentist nightmares) and said, "Nee jurda Chungwah whah (you know Chinese language)." I nodded. He shook hands with me and shouted, "You ding hao pungyo (you good friend)." He then explained to his fellow coolie the situation. The latter responded with great jubilation, and both began repeating the address we gave them. I climbed into the vehicle and off we sped to the house of Soong.

We went city block after city block away from the Legation Quarter and street lights, or for that matter, lights of any kind. The blocks seemed to become miles as the poor coolies trotted along at a fast clip. I told them to take it easy. They were sweating in the frigid darkness but slowed down and wrapped their heavy sheepskin coats around their formerly bare shoulders. We were miles into a residential district with houses behind high masonry walls and not a light in sight. The night was clear but the moon was not up, so it was as dark as any night on the front lines. My buddy said it was a long distance, but he had only traversed it in daylight—he was as lost as I was. We just hoped the coolies weren't.

Shortly, they turned down a narrow *hutung* so lined with

walls that it looked like a tunnel in the dim light. They pulled up in front of an imposing gate, which was bordered by a snug entrance cover on the house, complete with benches sheltered from the elements. The coolies eased their vehicle shafts down, mopped their brows with a little white towel, and sat on the footboard as they pulled on their sheepskins. We paid them and they bowed and grinned, making many remarks about a Marine speaking Chinese as they trotted off in the darkness. "Boy, those guys think you're a linguist, Sledgehammer." "If they only knew how little I know," I replied.

Paul applied the knocker to the massive brass-studded door. Soon we heard someone on the other side open a little panel in the door. A coolie, or houseboy, peeped out and said (in Chinese) "residence of Soong Taifoo." ("Taifoo" translates as "doctor.") My buddy gave his name. We heard heavy bolts being drawn, the big door swung open, and the coolie bowed, greeting us with "Nee hao (hello)." We followed him along a short stone walkway, through glass-paneled doors, and into a small anteroom with a bench on each side and an electric lamp hung from the ceiling. The doors were protection against the cold. Then we entered the hallway of the house. The hall was dimly lit and had a carpet runner on the floor. We could see rooms opening off the hall. Overall, the dimensions were not large.

The houseboy ushered us through the first door on the left, and we entered the living room or parlor. It was toasty warm with a tall, slender, coke-burning stove in the center of the room. The furnishings were Chinese but arranged in a definite western or European style. The coolie went out and closed the door. We sat on a comfortable sofa and waited.

Shortly, the door opened and in walked Dr. Soong, Father Marcel, Madame Soong, and her sister, Anna. Dr. Soong, or Soong Taifoo, as he was always addressed, was a very dignified, quiet gentleman. He was about five feet, eight inches tall and very thin. Whenever I saw him he was wearing Western attire. His suits, always with a vest, were of high quality and his black shoes brightly polished (a sign of proper attitude among Marines). A crisp white shirt and dark necktie finished off his well-dressed appearance. He looked like an American or European professional man but for his Asian features. His hair was neatly cut, of rather short length, and his face clean shaven. I imagine he was about forty years old.

Only a few minutes conversation with Soong Taifoo left no doubt that he was a man of great intelligence and depth. Little wonder that he was head surgeon at the Peiping General Hospital. His conversation was unique. He was soft spoken but voluble and almost always spoke in French addressed to Father Marcel, who translated it into English for the rest of us. Madame Soong, or Margaret, as she preferred to be called, said to me on one occasion: "My husband makes me furious—I speak to him in Chinese and if Father Marcel is here, he answers me in French, which I do not know. And Father translates into English or Chinese what my husband said to me. He won't speak to me in our own language if Father is here. It makes me angry." Soong Taifoo, fluent in Chinese and French, knew no English.

Soong Taifoo and Father Marcel had met in Paris years before World War II while students at the Sorbonne—the former in medical school and the latter in oriental studies. They had not seen each other for many years after their student days, even though Father Marcel had been posted to China for his missionary work. I never knew anyone to speak in any language with such relish and obvious joy at the sound as Soong Taifoo spoke French. He did not speak in an affected manner but rather like a man who gloried in his ability to make beautiful music. Unfortunately, I knew no French at that time, but Father Marcel said he spoke the language perfectly and without a foreign accent. In the absence of Father Marcel, Soong Taifoo spoke polished Mandarin Chinese, the dialect of the educated refined classes in the Peiping area and what might be called standard Chinese. But compared to French, Soong Taifoo seemed to regard any Chinese dialect as fit only for coolies.

Margaret was a very attractive woman and a good bit younger than her husband. They had no children. They seemed to have a good marriage and quite loving toward each other, although both were reserved in any show of affection. Margaret was pretty, and she wore her hair curled and rather short. The fit of her clothes revealed that she had a figure that would have done credit to any chorus line. Usually, she wore the traditional long Chinese dress with the slit to the knee on both sides. They were typically of beautiful silk brocade and clung to her shapely body, accentuating her figure like a thin drape on a Greek statue. At times she wore western clothes like any stylish American woman. Unlike many Chinese women, she had full, shapely breasts. I was told on several occasions that earlier Chinese custom considered this an undignified trait, and girls' breasts were bound to reduce their development. Margaret spoke English well, although sometimes her syntax caused even the kind Father Marcel to laugh, which she took in good humor. She spoke softly and was quite witty.

Margaret seemed to be adding a few unwanted pounds, which did not bode well for her fine figure. She was getting a bit "full" in the face, and her tummy, in which she had apparently taken pride when younger, was not as flat as it had once been. But with her dark sparkling eyes, witty conversation, bright smile, and sweet disposition, a few extra pounds were barely noticed.

Anna, Margaret's younger sister, was also very pretty. She was about five feet, five inches tall and in her late twenties. Anna had a fine figure like Margaret but a more beautiful face and sweeter smile. She usually dressed like a stylish American woman in beautifully tailored clothes. Sometimes she wore the traditional Chinese dress—which she did with panache. She was more reserved than Margaret but a bright and witty conversationalist with a good command of English. She and Margaret had been educated in a fine Catholic school in Peiping and had learned fluent English from academically demanding British nuns.

Unfortunately, Anna was in the process of getting divorced from her Chinese husband. I was told he was a fighter pilot stationed in another province. Although the matter was rarely mentioned, I gathered he wanted the divorce. He was said to be quite egotistical. If he wanted to divorce Anna, he must have been a moron. They had a young son who, like his father, I never saw. Being a devout Catholic, Anna seemed to be a bit melancholy about the divorce and subdued at times, unlike her ebullient sister.

Father Marcel was a native of Belgium, in his forties, but he looked younger. He was a muscular, robust man—more like a Marine than a priest. He was about five feet, nine inches tall, broad shouldered, and barrel-chested. His arms were large and hard. I commented on his physical fitness and muscular build. He laughed and said the nearly ten years the Japanese interned him with other Europeans in Weischen Prison Camp were responsible for his physique. He was ordered to shovel coal and stoke a furnace or be bayoneted as a troublemaker. He said the hard physical labor had been a blessing in disguise, although at the time he realized he was no more than a slave to the Japanese, who considered his life worthless. Father Marcel was a handsome man. A bit balding, he was blond with blue-gray eyes. His nose was a bit long but thin and, like his face, finely proportioned. His cheeks were habitually rosy, particularly when we were outside in the cold. He had a wonderful smile that showed his perfect white teeth. His face always reflected a radiance born of a deep conviction that he was doing God's work and was at peace with himself. To Father Marcel, life was beautiful despite the misery and brutality he had suffered and observed. One felt better about everything just visiting with Father Marcel. He was one of the finest men I ever knew; I've never had a friend like him. He had a marvelous wit and wonderful laugh. I never heard him laugh longer or more heartily than the time Margaret asked him, in her frank manner, if I was a Christian even though I was a Presbyterian. He told her, "Of course, Gene is a Christian!" and continued to laugh. After that, I was treated more like a beloved brother than a good friend by the entire Soong family.

The one thing shared by all these wonderful people was an appreciation, more akin to devotion, for the music of Wolfgang Mozart. In the living room was the latest prewar model RCA large phonograph. The collection of recordings included all of Mozart's symphonies, many of his piano concertos, and numerous other works by him. There was also some Beethoven, but mostly Mozart.

We had liberty about three afternoons a week. We had to check in by 11:00 P.M. or midnight, I don't remember which. During weekends, we had most of the day on Saturdays and Sundays, unless we were scheduled for guard duty or patrols. I often went to a restaurant for supper and then to the Soongs's afterward. I told Father Marcel I was afraid I would wear my welcome out. He replied that I was always welcomed by the family and that we all had such a good time together, they missed me when I didn't come to see them. In my early visits Paul and I went together, but later he got interested in "going out on the town" with other buddies. But to me, the home and family of Soong Taifoo was my home away from home, and I was never lonely in Peiping.

One day a message was left for me and the OD that I was invited for supper at the residence of Soong Taifoo. I arrived about 5:00 P.M., and we all had a glass of port wine in the living room. Then Margaret went out and sent their servant for supper. He pedaled off into the cold darkness on his rickshaw. About fifteen minutes later, he knocked and came into the living room with a huge tray of food. Everything was in metal thermal containers. We had individual little tray tables, and he served us all. I was amazed at the efficiency of the whole procedure. No Americans had ever heard of "take out" meals from a restaurant. In Peiping it was an old custom, and they had it down to perfection. On a cold night with driving snow, we sat down to a tasty hot meal ordered by phone from a nearby restaurant. It was several years after the war before American restaurants perfected this now common practice.

After supper the coolie cleared away the dishes, which I was told he would shortly return to the restaurant. Like all peasants, he wore thick cotton-padded trousers and shoes, a sheepskin coat, and a sheepskin cap with ear flaps. The Chinese knew how to dress for winter weather. Father Marcel said he might mumble about returning the dishes but wouldn't be cold. Unlike most Chinese rich, and poor, this coolie was a bit surly—apparently for no good reason as he had a good job and wasn't overworked, like many of his compatriots.

Margaret cranked up the phonograph and put on a Mozart symphony. Soong Taifoo lit up his pipe, so I broke mine out and did likewise. We didn't talk much because we listened to that sublime music with full attention. Occasionally, someone would comment on a particularly beautiful passage and all would nod their assent and smile. It was the warmest setting and friendship I've ever known, Mozart speaking to six dear friends of three nationalities—Chinese, Belgian, and American.

After the symphony we conversed about many things in English, Chinese, and French—with much translating by Father Marcel. I have often regretted that I didn't know then what I know now about science and philosophy. I had but one year of college and three years Marine Corps education in amphibious assault and infantry combat—my intellectual education was to come after these years. That night, Soong Taifoo had the French philosopher René Descartes on his mind. I knew very little about him then—to my great regret. Father Marcel translated all of the conversation for me—what I comprehended fascinated me. This was a typical evening. Some nights the conversation centered on China's ancient past. As an American I was amazed at the recounting of historical events that occurred over a thousand years ago. All present were keenly interested in life in the United States and my boyhood and home. Soong Taifoo was very pleased that my father was a physician.

On another night the damper in the stove pipe, which went straight up through the ceiling, was stuck, so the houseboy was called in to fix it. He came in all bundled up from duties outside the house in his heavy winter clothes and thick leather mittens. Soong Taifoo told him what the problem was, and without hesitation, the coolie climbed upon a stool and then onto the hot stove and began working with the damper. (Father Marcel, as usual translated his comments for me.) Shortly afterward, the servant began to mop his brow and shift from one foot to the other and comment vigorously about how hot the room was. He threw off his sheepskin cap and coat and continued to expound on the heat in the room, which he couldn't understand. Father Marcel and the Soongs all exploded with laughter. In the meantime the damper was fixed. The coolie looked around at us puzzled and said, "I do not understand why the room is so hot and I am the only one to notice this." Father Marcel said to him, "Do you realize you have been standing on a hot stove all this time?" The coolie looked down at his feet. His shoes had been moist with snow but were now steaming. "Ah ook, boo hao!" he exclaimed as he jumped to the floor, dancing around in his hot shoes and laughing heartily at his own absentmindedness. He grabbed up his coat and hat and ran from the room, mopping his brow. Margaret commented in English, "I have always thought he is the dumbest person I ever knew." It had been a real circus, and the main actor was not offended by our laughter.

Most of my Saturdays were spent sightseeing. The most interesting trips in and around Peiping were with Father Marcel, Margaret, and Anna; Soong Taifoo spent long hours at the hospital and was rarely able to go with us. The Forbidden City was a tremendous museum of incredible beauty. Father Marcel knew every feature in it and expounded on it more precisely and thoroughly than any tour guide I ever saw. The vastness of time involved in Chinese history never ceased to amaze me. The various dynasties, invasions, defenses, civil wars, cultural developments, and changes seemed endless. Father Marcel knew it all like the back of his hand. Margaret and Anna were very knowledgeable about it all but not being as fluent in English as Father Marcel, deferred to him.

The one period they seemed to try to avoid, and would always try to change the subject, was the period of Confucius. It so happened that I had bought a fine book of all his works in

Chinese with English translation below. I read most of it in off-duty hours and it all seemed very wise, moral, and sensible to me. I asked Father Marcel why the Soongs, and a few other educated Chinese I had talked with, seemed to have such an aversion to such a moral, benign man. He readily explained that Confucius was seen as a philosopher around whom a religion grew up, and he preached maintenance of the status quo in ancient China, which stifled progress and progressive change. (From what I was to see in the postwar United States, "progress" was a mixed blessing, with its medical miracles, high standard of living, pollution, and environmental destruction—and a bit of Confucian moderation would be desirable.)

One day in the Legation Quarter, while window shopping with these friends, Margaret and Anna suddenly grabbed me by one arm and turned me around and began chatting about something in a shop window. It was obvious they were trying to divert my attention from something. So I turned back around in time to see a Chinese peasant woman walking along the sidewalk coming in our direction. Her feet had been bound in the ancient custom, and each was no bigger than my fist. This Margaret and Anna didn't want me to see—they were ashamed that their country had maimed children in this fashion. The poor woman walked with short mincing steps and was a pitiful sight. I saw several such cases in China, though mainly in villages outside the larger cities. To do more than become familiar with Chinese culture would require a lifetime—but it was all fascinating.

CHRISTMAS IN PEIPING

Christmastime was about the same as any other time over most of North China in 1945. The weather was bitterly cold; many people did not have enough to eat; and the Communists and Chiang Kai-shek's Nationalists were struggling with each other for control of the war-weary nation. Thousands of disillusioned Japanese soldiers and civilians were awaiting repatriation after losing a war they thought they couldn't lose. But to the men of the U.S. First Marine Division, Christmas 1945 in North China was very special. It was the first peacetime Christmas in a long while. For the same reason, it was a very special Christmas to the Europeans released from internment camps by the Japanese.

The First Marine Division's three infantry regiments, the First Marines, the Fifth Marines and the Seventh Marines, were stationed in Tientsin, Peiping, and Chinwangtao respectively. The battalions of the division's artillery regiment, the Eleventh Marines, were attached to the infantry regiments as they had been during combat—for no one knew what might come to pass. If after knocking off the Nationalist units in the area, the Communists decided to seize the three mentioned important cities, combat-weary Marines would be under fire again.

The First Marines and attached artillery in Tientsin and the Fifth with their artillery support in Peiping lived in considerable comfort, billeted in steam-heated buildings. It was a comfort broken only by occasional patrols and railroad-escort details through a countryside raided by "bandits," "guerrillas," bona fide Communists, or other threats.

The men of the Seventh Marines weren't so lucky in Chinwangtao, down where the Great Wall of China meets the sea. Many of them had to bivouac in pup tents in the snow—miserable enough to most anyone but particularly to these men, many of whom had lived in the steaming tropical heat of the South and Central Pacific islands for as much as two years or more. Furthermore, the "unfriendly troops" in the Seventh's area were more aggressive than they were around Peiping or Tientsin.

It was my great luck as a member of K/3/5 to enjoy the good life in Peiping. There had been times during the war when it was a dubious privilege to be a member of such a celebrated old regiment as the Fifth Marines—that is, when the high command would assign us some extremely hazardous mission with the assurance that the Fifth Regiment could do the job where others might fail. But all that, though fresh in our memories, was behind us, and the men were making the most of being back in civilization again.

Many of the Catholics from Peiping's foreign legations had been practicing Christmas carols for their first peacetime Christmas service, and Father Marcel invited me to go with him, promising it would be something special to hear. So I accepted.

The large church was poorly lit and very cold. The congregation was made up of Europeans and Chinese, and the place had the usual garlic odor that seemed to me to be an integral part of the air in any building in Peiping. The choir consisted of Europeans. The carols were in Latin accompanied by a massive, deep-throated, melodious pipe organ. The choir sang the hymns as I think angels would. The members of the congregation were stately, graceful, and possessed that air of serenity seen in people who had survived dangers and deprivation, thankful the war was over and that they were delivered from the enemy. I have often thought that those carols were as different from the tinny, commercialized American versions as a Mozart sonata from a jazz song. Father Marcel was obviously very proud of the program and delighted that it pleased my Presbyterian ears.

On Christmas Day I went to divine services in Peiping's little English church. It was a small white wooden building with a picket fence. The Japanese had used the churchyard as a coal yard and had removed all the heating equipment from the building.

I sat in my great green overcoat on a hard upright pew that would have given a Pilgrim a backache and listened to one of the finest sermons I've ever heard. The minister was a robust Scot with a bushy black moustache. He wore a black broadcloth suit and a massive gold watch and chain. He spoke with a heavy burr and in a vigorous, dynamic manner. The sermon contained numerous favorable comments concerning the presence of the First Marine Division in Peiping. The main theme, however, concerned the relief and happiness of his congregation, back in their own church after years of internment by the Japanese.

The congregation comprised people of all ages. They had that thoroughly English look about them. They were courteous but gravely reserved. All were dressed in heavy tweeds and looked undernourished and pale, as did all the people I saw who had been interned by the Japanese.

Accompanied by the melodious pipe organ the Japanese had somehow overlooked in their quest for scrap metal, the congregation sang Christmas carols with charm and dignity. They would have done justice to Westminster Abbey. There was that same quality of relief arising from the sensation of being *free* again that I had heard in the Catholic service the previous night. I thought, if I had to be so far away from home and family this Christmas, at least I was sharing a deeply moving spiritual experience with exceptional people.

The Call of Duty

One night when on stand-by guard duty, I was sitting on my bunk reading Confucius (the Chinese in Peiping pronounced his name "Kung-foo tzee"). Three visitors entered and introduced themselves. They were well-dressed Italians in civilian clothes. All three were big, robust, dark-haired, handsome young men just out of Japanese internment camps. They told me in fluent English that they were Italian Marines and part of their legation's guard detachment in prewar days. Duty in Peiping then had been the best there was. They were not imprisoned until Italy switched sides to the Allied cause in 1943. So they had not suffered under Japanese captivity as much as some other nationals in Peiping. These men honestly seemed to have no loyalty to Mussolini at all and said they did not want a Hitler-type dictatorship in Italy. They seemed to be patriotic about their country, but not Il Duce.

Now the three were waiting for transportation home. In the meantime they were enjoying their freedom. One had a small concertina and said that they would like to sing some Italian songs for us. By this time, several K Company men had come in and greeted them. Our three visitors sang beautifully, like they were all professional opera singers. (One buddy told me later they were good because it was in their blood.) They sang selections from well-known Italian operas and numerous folk songs—all in Italian. The concertina gave it an air of authenticity; we all clapped and cheered. When the singers finished, we thanked them and asked them to come back, which they did several times while I was in Peiping. They told us with great sincerity that they had great admiration for U.S. Marines. We certainly enjoyed their visits.

We were ordered to prepare for a full regimental parade several days hence. It was to honor the Nationalist Chinese leader, Generalissimo Chiang Kai-shek. We were to parade in full combat gear in dungarees. As the weather was cold, we would all wear our longhandles. All troops "turned to" and began scrubbing 782 gear (that is, our web belts, straps, and everything attached to them), cleaning weapons, and generally squaring away their belongings.

None of us had ever seen Chiang but were familiar with his leadership against the Japanese in World War II and his current fight against Mao Tse-tung and his Communist forces.

Usually the troops grumbled and beat their gums about being on parade. But this one was considered an honor for the Fifth Marine Regiment, so I heard little complaining. It was considered an historic event.

The night before the parade, a sergeant came into the squadroom and called for me. I went to him and asked, "What's up?" He answered, "You won't parade tomorrow because the lieutenant wants you to go on a coal-buying detail for the battalion QM because you speak some Chinese. This Chink coal merchant will cheat us unless someone is there who can speak the lingo and check up on him. Report to the OD's office at the main gate at 0800, and he'll show you the truck and driver you are to accompany." All I could say was, "OK, Sarge." And so ended any participation in the historic parade.

Early next morning I bundled up in longhandles, sweatshirt, canvas leggings, wool green overseas cap, dungarees, and leather wool-lined gloves. It was a cold day and a bit windy. I took my pistol belt and two canteens of water. I reported to the OD's office at the legation's main gate. "Sledge," he said, "You are to be on the coal detail to be sure we aren't cheated. Speak the language, eh?" "A little, sir," I replied. I really didn't think I knew enough to do the job. "Well, I'm sure it's enough to keep tabs on the coal weight," he concluded. He gave me two sheets of paper on a clipboard. One was in English and stated the total weight and size or grade of pieces of coal ordered. The other was a duplicate order in Chinese. "Watch these merchants, they'll cheat us if you don't. A driver and his assistant will be along in the truck. They are both old rifle company Marines, wounded on Okinawa and transferred to the motor pool. So you'll be in good company. Don't take any nonsense from anybody in that coal yard." "Yes, sir," I said and saluted. The truck drove up and I went out and hopped in. My two companions were amiable old salts and also Southerners—so we got along fine. They grumbled about the detail because it would mean that after they delivered the coal they'd have a helluva job cleaning up their truck.

We drove on out through Chien Men (one of the huge main gates in Peiping's wall) to the railroad tracks. We passed sooty, grimy warehouses and other buildings. Everything looked like it had been built in the early nineteenth century, huge wooden warehouses with slate or rusting corrugated-iron roofs. We came to a high, brick-walled area with massive wooden doors with a number painted on. "This is the place," said the sergeant. The corporal turned to enter the gate and sounded the horn. A face appeared at the little peep aperture. It was shut and we heard a voice bellowing orders to open the gates. Timbers were removed from brackets, and we were signaled to drive into the coal yard. The wall was so old our truck could barely get through the narrow opening.

Suddenly about ten to twelve Chinese peasants rushed over from across the railroad tracks and started trying to squeeze themselves past the slowly moving truck and the wall into the coal yard. They all appeared to be teenagers. They wore thick dark blue or black cotton-padded coats and pants and their faces and hands were smeared with coal dust. From their facial features, they weren't a bad looking lot, just terribly poor.

Several squeezed on in past the truck—a very dangerous thing because they could have been injured. The driver was yelling at them in English to get back or they might get hurt. I was yelling the same thing in Chinese. But the coal yard manager was rushing around screaming like a maniac and ordering his four coolies to push them out the gate. Most coolies seemed to get excited in any crisis, and they were howling like banshees and pushing the gate shut as the trucks came through. The peasants who got in immediately started throwing large chunks of coal over the wall to their friends outside. The manager was threatening them with a shovel and then started kicking the ones he knocked down. I ran over and jerked the shovel away from him and threatened to hit him. The driver jumped out of the truck, grabbed him by the collar, and shook him like a rat. I threw a few pieces of coal over the wall as the coolies herded the other peasants out and shut and barred the gate. At first the manager was mad as a hornet with us, but I waved the invoices at him and he began to grin. He whined about those people stealing his coal. Bedlam had prevailed for a short while, and the manager complained he was only a poor honest man. I pointed to the invoices and said "Quai! Quai (hurry, hurry)!" The coolies came over, and he went to an old platform scale on wheels.

Most of what I saw done in China was slow and done by hand, as though there was endless time for the job. The coolies put a round basket about six inches deep onto the platform scale and then began shoveling coal into it. They were supposed to shovel a certain weight into the basket and then carry it by hand over to the truck and pour it into the truck bed. "Christ, we'll be here for a week at this rate," exclaimed the driver. I checked the scale each time and jotted the weight down in a notebook. The first basket was underweight, and the manager told the coolies to dump it into the truck. I stopped him and as best I could told him he was cheating us on weight. He began to argue—I had seen some Chinese arguments and knew they were always long-term episodes. I cursed him, which gave him a shock, and told him we wouldn't put up with any more cheating. So he immediately became obsequious and said it was a mistake. Every time I got stumped for the meaning of a word he naively helped me. The rascal tried the same cheating on the next four or five baskets, and I bawled him out—he only grinned and claimed it was a mistake. The sergeant turned to his buddy and said, "Get me the Tommy outta the truck." The corporal did so. The sergeant loaded a clip of ammo into the submachine gun with a loud click, pointed the muzzle at the manager's face, and said, "Sledgehammer, tell this bastard if he tries to cheat us again, I'll kill him." I translated what he said. The manager was shaking with fear, but we had no more cheating. When the truck was loaded, the sergeant drove back to battalion to unload. The corporal, the Tommy, and I were to await his return for another load.

Each time the truck left or returned, the same peasants rushed in as soon as the gate opened and pandemonium broke loose as before, with the manager kicking and screaming. The corporal and I were so disgusted with that paragon of business ethics that we threw as much coal over the wall as we could while he was distracted by the fracas. After his attempt at cheating, we saw no wrong in throwing as many lumps of coal over the wall as we could.

When we finally finished getting the ordered weight of coal, I gave the manager the invoice in Chinese. He was all smiles, grinning and shaking hands with us. We boarded the truck and the coolies opened the gate. As we drove out, the coal-seeking peasants rushed in and pandemonium broke loose again. As we looked back, the manager and his coolies had their hands full ejecting peasants from the premises while others rapidly threw coal over the wall. Some waved goodbye to us and grinned as though we had been allies against an oppressor. Peasants outside the wall were busily picking up chunks of coal and filling sacks. There were about twenty of these poor people trying to get enough coal to warm them against a harsh winter. There never seemed to be any possibility of calling police to establish order. Such disorder and poverty in China in 1945 were common wherever you looked.

As we drove back to Engua Foo at about noon to drop me off, we passed the big parade ground. The regiment was passing in review, the band was playing, and we could see Chiang on the reviewing stand. The driver stopped, and we watched across the big field as the different battalions of the Fifth Regiment and several artillery batteries of the attached units of the Eleventh Regiment rolled by pulling 105mm howitzers. They all looked the peak of precision, both infantry and artillery. We all agreed they were in step and looked sharp. Despite a rather bizarre morning, we did get to see the parade.

RETURN OF THE RUSSIAN

Several days latter, Val came by our squad bay. No one was glad to see this strutting person again. However, he said he was planning a big party with some "nice" Russian girls and plenty of vodka at the Moskva Club. Several of the men perked up at this enticing announcement and crowded around Val, pumping him with questions. He said the occasion for the party was to celebrate the victory by him and several of his men in taking a railroad station from some armed Japanese who held it illegally. He then treated us to a bit of profound wisdom, saying that one had to have the right connections in Peiping to get a party put on. He said the vodka would be free and that he knew all these girls, and they only slept with friends of his so they were not promiscuous; there was no need to worry about VD. The men were elated and began to make plans for the big party at 5:00 P.M. two days hence. Val expounded on the beauty of each of the women who would attend his party. "What a deal!" whispered one of my buddies to me. "Are you going, Sledgehammer?" I answered that he should know that Val was a fake and the biggest liar in North China but that I would go just to prove that point to myself and would bail out early. I told him he'd realize it too when VD hit him a few days after the party. These women were obviously Russian whores.

On the evening of Val's party, about six of us went by rickshaw to the Moskva Club several blocks away. It was a bit rundown but probably had been a fine-looking place in prewar years. Val had reserved a large round table with a spotless white tablecloth; it was loaded down with bottles of vodka, glasses, and dishes of various condiments. He greeted us in a loud voice and commented on how handsome we looked in our green wool uniforms. He introduced us to six or seven women friends. All had blond hair, apparently out of a bottle, and unpronounceable Russian names. They were delighted to see us and were excessively demonstrative of their admiration for U.S. Marines. None were in the least bit attractive. All had square faces, were painted up like mannequins, and were on the plump end of the weight scale for their height. The vodka was soon flowing. I ordered a bottle of Chinese beer, "Oah sing sing," or five-star beer, because I did not like vodka. Val was shouting orders to two pasty-faced, square-headed young Russians in white jackets and black trousers. They did a good job, but it was obvious they considered Val a big-mouthed phony, as I did. The girls all spoke English with a heavy accent, and their conversation was as thick and ignorant as one would expect. All began by professing that, like Val, they hated Reds and could never return to Russia since their forebears had been Czarists. Val added a call for a toast to Mother Russia without the Reds.

There was much conviviality, and one girl asked Val to tell us of his famous exploit at the provincial railroad station. Val described in detail how he, as head railroad detective commanding twenty Chinese puppet-government troops, had surrounded the brick building miles from Peiping. They had endured great hardship by standing in ankle-deep, cold swamp water before all was ready for the "attack." They caught the Japanese "detachment" completely by surprise, and when they refused to surrender, Val gave the order to open fire. The Japanese got off a few rounds before they were shot down to a man. Due to his superior leadership, he didn't lose a man. He then muttered, "War is dangerous and terrible." After this profound observation, I asked Val how many Japanese were in the "garrison." He answered four riflemen and a telegraph operator. Every Marine burst forth with loud guffaws and howls of laughter. One said, "Sonny, you don't know what war is!" I asked Val if he had ever been under shellfire, and he said no. I told him if he ever was, he'd really know what war was all about. His ego and bombast were irrepressible, and what we said didn't even make sense to him.

My buddies consumed enough vodka that the women began to seem very desirable, and they began to pair off with them and leave the table, walking down a dark hallway with much giggling on the part of their newfound friends. One of my buddies whispered, "Sledgehammer, which one are you going with?" "None," I replied, "and if you don't want vd you better leave 'em alone too." "Aw, Val said they're nice girls," he protested. "If you believe that lying bum you're drunker than I thought," I replied. I left without a word to our genial host, went outside where the bracing cold felt refreshing, hailed a rickshaw, and headed for the home of Soong Taifoo. I was greeted warmly by genuinely nice people. Supper was ordered, and we had a fine family evening.

The next day the partygoers all had terrible hangovers and groaned at the brisk PT we were run through before chow. They all told me what a great party I had missed and that the girls were wonderful and affectionate.

After several days, the incubation period for various forms of VD had elapsed, and all Val's guests came down with severe cases. The mere mention of his name brought forth streams of profanity and condemnation of that "lying loud-mouthed little bastard." To my knowledge, no one ever returned to visit their lady friends at the Moskva Club.

About two weeks later, Val exhibited the poor judgment of coming by one evening to "see his Marine buddies." One grabbed him and shook him like a rag doll and told him he'd whip his ass if it weren't for the fact he'd land in the regimental brig for starting a fight. Val beat a hasty departure. I saw him on the street several times before I left for home, but he never returned to our squad bay.

RUMORS AND CHANGES

Some of the older veterans began rotating Stateside on the point system. A certain number of points were awarded each man for each battle star, Purple Heart, decoration, and month overseas. Old friends were jubilant to be going, but it was hard to leave friends who had shared the perils and hardships of combat. Due to the uncertainties of China's civil war, all who left felt like escapees from the unknown. To have survived the Pacific War was prodigious luck, not to be stretched thin in chaotic China of 1945.

Replacements came in to take the places vacated by the old salts leaving. Among the first in K/3/5 was a gunnery sergeant who had served throughout World War II in the States. No one ever understood how he reached such high rank and never served overseas. If we got into any kind of fight with the Communists, the last thing we needed was a greenhorn company gunny when that position was so critical under fire. The new gunny was keenly aware of his lack of experience and our resentment of the fact, and he carried a chip on his shoulder about it. He resented our combat experience as much as we resented his lack of it. This guy could foul up an operation in the field if he didn't know his stuff. He handled all this like an immature boot by trying to play the part of a tough guy. Needless to say, this just made the veterans even less confident in him.

If a Marine came into Engua Foo, he had to check in at the Main Gate with the OD or sergeant of the guard, and he better not show any indication of being under the influence of alcohol. Nor could he bring alcoholic beverages on post. Entry by the Main Gate or coming over the high brick wall were the only ways to get in; obviously, coming over the wall, a tough obstacle, would result in immediate arrest and stiff disciplinary action if caught.

One wintry day at twilight, I checked out and hailed a rickshaw to go to the home of Soong Taifoo. Just then, one of our trucks pulled up to let off about a dozen Marines returning from a work detail. The new gunny was standing in front of the gate inspecting each of us before we went on liberty. The sergeant of the guard had already done this as we checked the liberty roster inside the gate—this was s.o.p.—standard operating procedure. But this gunny wanted to demonstrate how G.I. he was—that is, a strict disciplinarian. Of course, we had to wait there and stand inspection again because of his rank—cussing him under our breath all the while.

Just as I got in the rickshaw, "String Bean" appeared, returning early from liberty. He was drunk as an owl. As he paid off his rickshaw coolie, he came up rolling and lurching like an old salt on his "sea legs" negotiating the deck in a heavy sea. As he came tacking toward the gate, all the men detrucking and those of us leaving on liberty yelled cheers to String Bean. He acknowledged our greeting with a wobbly salute and a broad grin. String Bean was about six feet tall and weighed about 135 pounds. He was an old K Company man who had been seriously wounded on Peleliu during a disastrous attack on the Five Sisters hill mass, taking a rifle bullet about two inches above his navel. By some miracle he survived, and when "in his cups," he invariably insisted on pulling up his shirt and pointing out to all within earshot the neat round scar as "my second navel—I'm the only Marine what's got two." He was good natured and friendly, drunk or sober. String Bean was a good Marine and brave as any in combat; we all liked him very much.

The new gunny, a husky man, grabbed String Bean by the lapels of his heavy green wool overcoat, shook him violently, and growled, "What the hell do you mean returning from liberty in this condition, you drunk bastard." As though on cue, all the men on the truck and those of us just leaving started yelling, "Lay off String Bean!" and continued to shout curses at the gunny to pick on somebody his size. The gunny loosed String Bean and yelled, "Knock it off, you people—just because you've been in combat you think you won the war!" That did it. We lost all respect for him right then. The OD, a combat veteran and a popular lieutenant, heard all the ruckus, and he and the old-salt sergeant rushed out thinking there was a riot brewing. Everyone got quiet, and that innocent "who me" look appeared on every face in the dim light. The OD asked us what the problem was. Someone spoke up and said, "Aw, the gunny was roughing up String Bean, sir." The OD told String

Bean to go with the sergeant of the guard, and he went over to the gunny and said something. Then he told us to disperse. That ended one of the most humiliating episodes I ever saw a Marine NCO bring upon himself. We didn't think we were superior because we were combat veterans, but we observed discipline, followed orders, and respected our officers and NCOs unless they acted improperly.

Unfortunately, at this period the Marine Corps, like the other armed services, looked on alcohol consumption as a manifestation of manliness, an attitude that fortunately changed in later years. From what I experienced, a Marine had his hands full with his duties and meeting the demands of discipline. Alcohol beyond one or two beers caused the users and their superiors most of the conduct problems that occurred.

My father had taught me at an early age of the behavioral and addictive problems associated with an overindulgence of alcohol, so I always limited myself to one beer and stayed out of trouble. To me, the difficulties caused by anything but a small amount of alcohol were not worth it.

When first in China, some of my buddies insisted I "learn to drink" with them. I'd have one beer and no more. They finally gave up, and I never condemned their behavioral preferences. They always openly respected my attitude and often said they envied me because, when drunk, they sometimes did things they later deeply regretted or that got them into trouble of some sort. I never manifested any "holier than thou" attitude regarding my habits, and my buddies realized I had simple practical reasons, which they respected. I respected them because they were the finest men I ever knew and fine Marines.

Interior guard duty was rotated throughout the companies as it had been on Pavuvu. In Peiping there were very practical reasons for guard duty in the legation. There was always the possibility that Communist agents or simple thieves might get over the wall and cause problems. The guard posts were at the gate, near certain areas within the wall, or outside of certain supply buildings.

One afternoon the gunny called me to the guard room, where he was ensconced behind a desk like he was the skipper. "Sledge," he said, "I'm making up the guard roster for next week and I want you to be corporal of the guard." "I'm not a corporal, Gunny, I'm a PFC," I replied. "Well, I'm making you acting corporal for this guard duty." "Gunny, I don't want to be acting corporal; I don't want the responsibility unless I get the stripes and pay for a promotion." I had seen enough of the acting-NCO status during the war and had had it handed to me whether I liked it or not. Often it entailed heavy responsibility and never any compensation. Then when the next replacement draft came in there were always NCOs who took over the job and gave you the orders. I have no proof, but it seemed to me during and after the war that more inexperienced Stateside NCOs were sent to our division and the combat-wise old salts remained for years without any promotion in rank. Some PFCs had been platoon leaders on Okinawa. In some of the divisions formed later, men I'd known in boot camp were rapidly promoted to fill NCO positions.

Due to the point system, I would be sent home soon, so my eagerness to perform duties above my actual rank had been worn out by this time. As I expected, the gunny blew his stack, ranted and raved, and promised he would assign me the most undesirable post in the legation. I only shrugged as he shouted, "You Company ole timers have a rotten attitude—dismissed!" I walked out perfectly satisfied with the turn of events in the matter.

Guard duty in the compound, with its well-lighted streets

and buddies continually passing and exchanging greetings, was simple and easy compared to that on Pavuvu. There, one post I had was "guarding" a stack of empty 55-gallon oil drums in a low, swampy, mosquito-infested area about ten feet below the ground level of the rest of the island. There was no logic in having a guard post there. It was just one of those cases where a certain number of posts were needed to fill out the roster even if it meant guarding a palm stump.

It was after Peleliu, and listening to land crabs crawling about, the pounding surf only a few feet away, made many of us dread the place on inky dark nights. It was the loneliest place I ever saw, and for four hours I waited for my relief and couldn't help watching behind me and listening intently for Japanese infiltrators when no Japanese had been on Pavuvu in years. But I had formed survival habits on Peleliu that I would never break.

No Military Police company was assigned to Peiping. However, an MP force was needed to patrol the streets and see that Marines stayed out of trouble. The high command assigned the job to L/3/5. The L Company men got tired of hustling drunk buddies back to the brig, but it suited the rest of the battalion. We dreaded the day the MP job might rotate to our company.

L Company was a rifle company we had fought shoulder to shoulder with during at least two campaigns. Those men did a good job, and we respected them because they were front-line Marines, many of whom we knew personally. Regular MPs we regarded as rear-echelon types who were assigned rear-area jobs directing traffic far behind the front line. They resented front-line Marines because they knew how we felt about them, and they often tried to show their authority and push people around. Not the L Company MPs, however. Sometimes they had no choice but to apply force in handling misbehaving infantry Marines they knew personally who were drunk and rowdy. But they were fair.

There was an old Marine Corps saying that some duty was "as fouled up as a Chinese fire drill" when it was not snappily executed. Once I actually saw this demonstrated. A buddy and I got twenty-four-hour passes to travel to the other side of Peiping to see various historic places there. We spent the night at a Marine Corps facility that had recently been established for such use. It had a large brick-paved court, a barracks, and a mess hall, enclosed by a high wall. It must have been some sort of military facility in former days. The whole place was neat and clean as a pin. There was a small Marine unit, about a platoon, billeted there permanently, but I never knew what outfit it was. From the looks of their 782 gear (which looked new and not at all "salty"), I assumed they were not infantry.

We had evening chow in the mess hall on long tables covered with white tablecloths. It was far better fare than that served in our mess hall. As we finished chow, a gong sounded repeatedly and rapidly. Shouts of "Fire!" rang out from the galley; an officer came through ordering all troops outside on the double. My buddy and I pulled on our overcoats and headed for the courtyard. There a condition of utter chaos prevailed. A Chinese fire company, with uniforms and firemen's helmets, had rolled in a hand-operated wagon-wheeled pumper and were unrolling hose. They were all shouting at the top of their lungs, and some seemed to run aimlessly back and forth accomplishing nothing. On each side of the pumper, about six to eight firemen were working a long handle up and down. No water was in the tank, so none squirted out of the nozzle held by an important-looking individual in a fancy uniform who was bawling orders to everybody. The long auxiliary hose was unrolled by one group, who attached one end to a fireplug near the wall. Another group attached the other end of the hose to another fireplug across the courtyard, and both groups shouted triumphantly as they turned on the water at their respective ends—and water under pressure flowing in opposite directions in the same hose caused it to burst violently. The resulting geyser spouted about twenty feet in the air and fell, soaking the energetic shouting firemen.

Smoke was drifting out of a window at the end of the mess hall. A Marine corporal from permanent personnel ran up and ordered his men to form a bucket brigade from the horse trough in the courtyard to the galley. They used their steel helmets (minus liners) as buckets. My buddy and I got in line and helped pass the helmets along. In no time the Marine cooks had doused the fire with water-filled helmets as the Chinese fire company danced around shouting and triumphantly cheering each other and their chief. Every Marine in the place was laughing out loud. It never seemed to occur to the proud firemen that they had absolutely nothing to do with extinguishing the fire. It took them about an hour to reassemble their equipment and proudly march out of the courtyard as we shouted "Ding hao!" and waved and cheered—and mostly laughed. The firemen waved, smiled, and shouted "Ding hao!" The whole affair was the funniest unrehearsed comedy I ever saw.

Returning to the battalion after my sightseeing trip, I found to my disgust that my name was on the guard roster for duty the next night. It wasn't my turn, but the gunny was really out for revenge because I had refused the acting corporal job. The next evening I reported to the guard room and was assigned a post along the wall in an almost deserted, dimly lit area of the legation. Few people passed by day and nearly no one by night. There was a low wall enclosing what had been a beautifully planted English formal garden. It had been neglected during the war years, and the shrubbery was quite overgrown now—a good potential hiding place for unauthorized persons.

Shortly after I was posted by the corporal of the guard and he and the others had moved to the next post, a person approached me out of the garden gate. I challenged him and demanded the password. He complied properly, and a voice said, "Sledgehammer, I gotta talk to you." To my surprise, it was the Marine from the nearby guard post. I asked him what he was doing leaving his post. He said excitedly, "I've got this girl and I need you to warn me if the corporal comes back." "What the hell are you talking about—you are on guard duty!" He came up leading a small Chinese woman—or girl—wrapped in a Marine overcoat with a fore-and-aft cap pulled down over every part of her head but her eyes. She was "Suzie," he told me, and he had gotten over the wall in the darkness and was going to take her into the garden for some loving. He asked me to challenge anyone loudly who passed my post headed toward his while they were in the bushes. This, he explained, would warn him and give him time to hide Suzie and get back to his post. I bawled him out for taking such a stupid chance with Marine Corps discipline. "You desert your post to get in the bushes with a Chinese whore, and if you're caught it'll either be a firing squad or the rest of your life busting rocks at Mare Island Naval Prison." "Aw, Sledgehammer, I won't get caught—you can have a go with Suzie, I'm paying her. Suzie, this Sledgehammer, he me ding hao pungyo." Suzie grinned at me with as much allure as an alley cat. I only groaned at his stupidity and rolled my eyes. Even all bundled up, Suzie was obviously skinny as a broomstick and probably about fifteen years old, one of those poor unfortunates sold into literal slavery by a poverty-stricken family who couldn't afford to feed her. The many manifestations of poverty in postwar China were as cruel as they were common. "You dumb bastard, get the hell outta here before you get us both in trouble," I growled. "OK, OK, Sledgehammer, we're going, but remember, sing out loud and clear at anybody that comes along." "Shove off!" I snarled.

I was nervous about my own skin if his stupid plan was discovered. Corporals of the guard had a reputation for being "cagey birds" about any irregularities on a guard post. The Marine and Suzie disappeared into the darkness toward the garden. He told me the next day that he had a fine time with her. One of his buddies, by prearranged plan, came by and slipped her over the wall along where a big tree limb hung over it. I told him he was a lucky gambler—he just grinned. This man had a good combat record, but Marine Corps discipline was hard and relentless about everything—particularly guard duty and leaving one's post for any reason.

A NEW YEAR IN NORTH CHINA, 1946

We had several snowstorms in January, and the Forbidden City was particularly beautiful with a blanket of white powdery snow.

Late one afternoon a buddy and I were walking along the sidewalk scraping up snow and throwing snowballs at trees and at each other. Suddenly, as we passed a portion of low wall about five feet high in the rear of the U.S. Legation, we saw a tempting target moving along just above the top of the wall. It was an officer's frame green wool cap with a shiny visor. We couldn't resist! We both took careful aim, allowed for lead, and hurled our snowballs. Direct hit! by one or both—the cap flew off in a shower of snow. The gentleman-owner uttered a loud curse. There was a pause as he apparently retrieved his hat. Then we heard him cursing as his feet pounded the bricks toward a gate to catch the criminals. We took off at a dead run in the gathering darkness. The gentleman whose dignity we had offended never realized in which direction we fled, so he did not give chase.

One night during a dust storm, a buddy and I traversed the sidewalk past the open main gate of the German Legation. There stood a Chinese puppet-army soldier at parade rest beneath a dim light in the arch of the main gate. As we approached, he glanced at us, and we both said, "Hello, friend," in clear Mandarin Chinese, understood by all Chinese regardless of which dialect they spoke themselves. He popped to attention, then port arms, as we passed. After we disappeared from his view in the dusty haze along the sidewalk, we heard the crack of a rifle bullet passing over our heads. It clipped off some twigs, which fell around us from the leafless tree above. Instantly , we took off at a dead run and didn't slow up until we rounded a walled corner. My buddy said in an irritated voice, "Why the hell did that crazy bastard fire toward us? We didn't threaten him in any way." "Those guys seem so trigger-happy and poorly disciplined they shoot at people for no reason," I answered. Our hearts were pounding—we had been shot at more than enough. We reported the incident to the OD when we came in at the Main Gate of Engua Foo. We never heard anything further about it, however. With all the different factions in the city, Peiping could be a dangerous place just walking down the street in 1946. Chinese sentries were notoriously unpredictable.

Every time we went out on the street, we were approached by one to several moneychangers. They wore long Chinese winter robes and, usually, an American-style felt hat. They carried large briefcases filled with Chinese money to exchange for U.S. currency. There were two types of Chinese currency —terribly confusing but each apparently considered sound money—

CNC (Chinese National Currency) and another type, the name of which I have forgotten. The moneychangers would rush up smiling and saying, "Chanjah money pwease," and then state their rate in Chinese dollars for "one gold" (one U.S. dollar). It always turned into a bargaining session, with each money-changer trying to offer the best rate and the Marine trying to get the best rate he could.

One rate I recall was one gold for 2,000 CNC dollars, but rates changed daily. Before I left, inflation had increased so that we all carried large leather wallets to hold the oversized Chinese money. I often saw the hilarious sight of a Marine who had changed some U.S. money into many small-denomination CNC bills riding down the street tossing money from his rickshaw and being followed by a horde of Chinese, all yelling loudly trying to scoop up the money.

In about the middle of February, I was told to square away my gear to leave the next day for home. I really didn't get excited because I had been disappointed too many times by circumstances to feel that I was actually going home. Sure enough, I was told the next day there would be a delay because, in checking the records, one man was found to have one more point than I.

About this time, we were summoned by companies to the post theater to hear a Marine major speak on the fact that combat veterans in China were rotating home at such a slow pace because U.S. troops all over the globe were demanding immediate transport home. It seemed to us that (as we expected) noncombat-support troops protested the loudest, from what news reports stated. The reporters rarely differentiated between those troops who had risked their lives in combat units and those who had served in cushy support service. A surprisingly large number of news people didn't seem to know the difference between combat and noncombat troops; to them, a soldier was a soldier. But we could determine these differences when units were identified. Of course, combat correspondents were as aware of the differences as we were.

The major explained that we Marines had a critical mission in North China. Duty came first, but men would be sent home by the point system as ships became available. Several Marines jumped to their feet and stated that we were being exploited after so much combat service, while other troops with lesser service in safe places were going home. There was a general uproar of assent. I had never seen Marines react in this manner to anyone in authority. The major shed his formerly kind demeanor as he left the podium and strode across the stage. The ribbons on his chest indicated that he was an old salt and had seen hard service. The shouters, still standing, were "sailing pretty close to the wind" to be disrespectful to a man such as this major. He spun on his heel, pointed at those standing, and said in a stern voice: "You people are Marines—act like it! Sit down and knock it off! If you don't, you are guilty of insubordination." The shouters sat down or were pulled down by their buddies. Silence prevailed. The major repeated that we would be sent home as rapidly as possible. He said the Marine Corps was not insensitive to our record, but duty must be done. We were dismissed and filed silently out of the theater. We continued to beat our gums elsewhere and awaited our turns to go home.

The next afternoon, on liberty, I went through the huge ancient gate Chien Men into an area of very old Chinese shops. These shops were very small, with one or two clerks, and arranged along narrow *hutungs*. Each shop was very specialized and sold only such things as ancient Chinese armor and weapons, or small brass boxes, or fine silk robes. They were all very dimly lit with oil lamps as darkness came on. Nobody spoke a word of English. It was a fascinating area that I regretted not having found sooner. I bought a fine open-work brass pet-cricket box, some small vases, and silk handkerchiefs.

Just before it was time for me to report back from liberty, I entered a small shop stuffed with ancient Chinese arms and armor. My eye caught a fine recurved bow with a square quiver filled with arrows. The proprietor took it down and let me examine it carefully. The bow was very old—the type I had seen only in drawings of Cupid or ancient Mongols on horseback and in a movie about Marco Polo. It was only about four feet long, very stout, and backed with thin strips of polished horn. The craftsmanship was beautiful. The arrows were tipped with browned-steel, razor-sharp, broadhead points. They were held upright in slots in a wood-and-leather quiver—much like an elongated box. The feathers on the arrows were obviously old but in fine condition. It was a powerful weapon in its time. I bargained with the proprietor, and we struck up a deal—which was cheap by U.S. standards. My problem, however, was wrapping the bow and quiver so I could carry it aboard ship with all my gear when I went home. I told the shopkeeper this and that I would come back as soon as I could and purchase these fine antiques. He agreed. Much to my everlasting regret, events transpired so rapidly that I was never able to get back to that shop.

When I returned to my squad bay that night, to my astonishment it was as cold as the outside. My squad mates were all grumbling and cursing. While most of us were on liberty, an old buddy (whom I'll call Pete) had gotten roaring drunk, taken an entrenching-pick handle, and smashed out every pane of glass in the large window. The two men present had tried to subdue him, but when drunk, he would fight anybody near him like a wildcat. They called out the guard, who came in and brought Pete under control with billy clubs and threw him in the brig. The windows could not be fixed until next day. It was a cold night, and by morning snow had blown in onto many of our bunks.

Pete was a good Marine—good as any I ever knew in combat. We had been foxhole buddies many times on both Peleliu and Okinawa. He was a Gloucester veteran, brave, generous, fair, witty, and popular in K Company. However, when he drank, it was always too much, and invariably he became both belligerent and determined to smash any glass in sight. He was about my size but when drunk would fight anybody and everybody. Although old friends, we did not pull liberty together because we went our separate ways.

Next day, we fell out in full gear for 60mm mortar gun drill. The machine gunners and other K Company Marines also went through combat drills. It seemed so anticlimactic after the war. However, tensions were increasing in North China as the Communist forces became more aggressive against patrols and train guards. Several Marines in the division were killed by snipers. Although the Reds usually paid dearly for their attacks, casualties did not seem to bother them. As a result, we had to stay in fighting trim, like it or not. Each veteran was praying he would get home before he became a casualty in China's civil war.

That night I went on liberty, had a fine dinner at Tsui Hua Lo (Palace) Restaurant, and had a long visit with the proprietor, who had become a good friend. Chang Chow Chin spoke good English and ran the finest Chinese restaurant in the city. He entertained me for hours with stories of China's long history.

Pete was let out of the brig only to get into bigger trouble on his next liberty. He got drunk, went down the street to the White Front Cafe, and insulted one of the Chinese waitresses. The White Front was a nice place patterned after a traditional English tea room. The entire front of the place was enclosed by large windows with the muntins painted white. I had been there many times, and it was a very dignified and proper place—no catering to anyone who didn't conduct himself in the manner of a proper English gentleman. The Chinese proprietor had been very popular with the prewar legation Europeans. In fact, he conducted himself in a most English manner.

When Pete propositioned one of the Chinese waitresses, she told the proprietor. He asked Pete to leave. That set off Pete, who socked the unfortunate man. He then upended a tea table, jerked off one leg, and, using it as a club, threatened all the guests in the place. They naturally fled at the sight of this club-wielding, raging drunk. Then Pete proceeded to methodically "turn to" on the glass front of the White Front. He smashed out every last piece of glass in the place.

The MPs were summoned and L Company dispatched a squad to arrest Pete. One of them later told me they arrived to find Pete standing in the middle of the room and the place in shambles, with broken glass covering the floor. The employees were huddled in the kitchen, and the Chinese cook was prepared to defend himself with a meat cleaver. The MP corporal, who knew Pete, asked him to surrender peacefully. Pete answered by swinging at him with his club. He was now rested after the exertion of smashing up the place, but fortunately the old-salt corporal ducked and planted a blow on top of Pete's head with his billy club. It might as well have been a blow from a flyswatter, one of the squad told me later. "We didn't want to hurt him, Sledgehammer, but the fool was raging drunk and we had to bring him in," the Marine told me. A brawl ensued between Pete and the entire squad. They finally had to beat him down to the deck with their clubs to take him into the brig. The Marine I spoke with said, "I've known that guy about two years, but never saw him drunk before. He was wild—I never saw anything like it. I'm sorry we had to beat the hell out of him, but he wouldn't stop fighting." Pete was patched up by a corpsman and put in the brig on cake and wine (bread and water).

SAYING GOODBYE

I got word by way of a buddy in battalion headquarters that another group of high-point men would soon leave for home and that I was on the list again. I got liberty and intended to go tell the Soong family and Father Marcel goodbye. First, I went by the brig to tell Pete goodbye. If he had stayed out of trouble, he would have been on his way home long before me since he was a three-campaign veteran.

The sergeant of the guard showed me to his cell and left us to talk through the bars. It was a strange sensation seeing an old friend locked in an iron cage like a wild animal. Pete was glad to see me and was as jovial as ever. We talked over old times awhile, and I expressed regret over his present predicament. Typical Pete, he grinned and said, "But, Sledgehammer, I had a helluva good time." What a guy. His face was a mess, swollen and bandaged. Both eyes were swollen almost shut, and he was a mass of bruises all over. I shook hands with him through the bars and we said goodbye. Then to my amazement he said, "Please, Sledgehammer, when you come in tonight slip me a quart of vodka, please. Nobody'll see you, honest, I've got to have it." "Ole buddy," I replied, "you know I'd do anything I could for you. But if you don't leave that stuff alone you'll never get out of the brig, much less get home." I could well imagine him drunk in the brig and no doubt beating up the OD. I said goodbye again and quickly left. It seemed that he had reached the point where he couldn't leave alcohol alone. It was truly a sad situation; he was a good Marine in combat and a close friend.

I had dinner at the Palace Restaurant and said my goodbyes to Chang and his amiable waiters.

The family of Soong Taifoo and Father Marcel were all glad to see me. We visited awhile, and then I told them I had to say goodbye because I would be leaving for home soon. Margaret hugged me and said I was a good boy. She gave me a beautiful white jade disc carved with bats with wings joining and their heads facing inward toward the Chinese character "Sho." This meant longevity. The spoken sound could also mean bat, thus the bat was the symbol for longevity. She said the roughly two-inch-diameter disc had been one of the buttons on her grand-mother's Mandarin coat. I said maybe I shouldn't take it, but Father Marcel whispered to me that she would be highly offended if I declined. Soong Taifoo, normally dignified and reserved, shook hands warmly as tears ran down his face, and he said, "Qui john egin Shih." Then he spoke in French to Father Marcel, who translated, "He said he is very sad you are leaving." Farther Marcel shook hands and said he was going to visit his mother in Belgium and then come to the States. He was confident we would see each other again. (Happily, we did just that after I got home—he came through Mobile and met my parents.) Anna walked out to the front gate with me and was crying. I held her hand and said goodbye. She threw her arms around me and kissed me on the mouth like we were more than friends. I thought it was just as well I was leaving when I was, but I was sorry her personal life was not good.

The Soongs had their coolie ride me back to Engua Foo. We said goodbye and I gave him a big tip. He almost danced a Chinese jig—if there is such a thing. The Soongs were some of the finest, most refined people I've ever known, who gifted me with a mixture of friendship and almost familylike affection.

What timing my farewells had been! When I got to my squad bay, a sergeant came by with a list and said, "Sledgehammer, have your gear squared away and ready to board a truck at the Main Gate, board for the railroad station at 0800 tomorrow morning—you are headed stateside." I was overjoyed; this time it was true! I made the rounds within K Company and the battalion saying goodbye to old buddies. It was difficult to do this with friendships forged in combat. But we all kept a stiff upper lip and acted jovial outwardly. Poor Hao Ching Foo shed tears, as I did, when we parted. He was a good little fellow. It depressed me to think of what would happen to all my Chinese friends when the inevitable day came of a Communist takeover of Peiping. Sadly, the Nationalists were losing the civil war.

With several K Company buddies, I boarded a truck at the Main Gate for the ride to the Peiping train station. I got one last glance at the fabulous Forbidden City and then at the huge fortress gate of Chien Men. What a remarkable place Peiping is, I thought.

We boarded the train for Tientsin, with the typical sight of Chinese civilians with luggage and children hanging on the outside or riding on top of the cars. PFC H. P. McQueen, an old K Company buddy and former farm boy from Wisconsin, and I sat together bundled in our green wool overcoats for the ride to Tientsin in unheated coaches. The trip was interesting and uneventful. The winter countryside was endlessly brown and dusty, with snow in some places and peasants visible in their thick cotton-padded clothes around farms and little villages. I spoke briefly to some Chinese in the railroad station at Tientsin. These were about the last conversations in Chinese I had.

We were transported to Taku, where we boarded the attack transport USS *Wakefield*. An officer carefully checked our names on a list.

Most of the men from the Fifth Marines were billeted in a forward compartment about three decks down below. As usual, it was a chore stowing our gear in the space between the narrow racks that served as bunks. My rack was about the fourth up from the deck, and I had to be careful not to step on the hands or feet of sleepers as I climbed up and entered my narrow low space. Our compartment had an I/3/5 corporal in charge. We all knew him well. He was a good-natured New Yorker of Italian descent and an old combat veteran. He never ordered us around but quietly told us what had to be done and we did it. We did it to keep our compartment ship-shape.

The officer in charge of the compartment was an amiable first lieutenant who had served in a Marine aircraft wing as the officer in charge of maintenance. He was easy to deal with and respected us as combat-infantry veterans. He voluntarily admitted the vast difference between his war and ours, and we respected him all the more for it.

Once during the voyage to the States, there was an inspection of our compartment by a Marine colonel. Each group of men stood at attention beside their row of racks. There was so little room, we were packed like sardines. The lieutenant said to the colonel as they passed us, "Colonel, you won't find any problems in this compartment inspection. These are old infantry Marines and they understand discipline." When the colonel finished his inspection, he said everything was in fine order and complimented the lieutenant and us. The lieutenant was so pleased he was almost giddy. The people in charge of our compartment left us alone as long as we kept things squared away, which we were used to doing anyway.

However, the ship's complement of seagoing Marines was another matter whenever we went topside. We all knew there were areas on every ship that were restricted to troop passengers and we acted accordingly. But these people went out of their way to constantly order us not to stand here or not to sit there. They yelled at us and ordered us about like we were recruits. It got so bad, our men began to curse them and ignore their orders. One old salt named Bruno, who was built like a gorilla and a genuine Brooklynite, told a seagoing Marine who was ordering us to move along the deck, "Knock it off you meathead or I'll throw youse over da side and give youse da deep six." The other man blushed and said he was going to get the officer of the deck. Bruno said he'd throw him over the side too. We began to joke about not sitting here or there but "Grab a skyhook, Marine."

It all came to a head one day quite near where I happened to be. The first lieutenant of the seagoing detail was complaining to one of our officers that we were undisciplined and would not follow orders. Our officer told him that was untrue and that we were the best-disciplined troops in the service but would not tolerate and need not be treated like green recruits. If it did not stop, he said, he'd report harassment to the ship's CO. From then on, the seagoing sentries left us alone.

The ship docked at Tsingtao on the Shantung Peninsula and took on veterans of the Sixth Marine Division headed home. In the harbor that night, we watched Chinese fishermen with cormorants with brass collars. The fishermen used these birds, relatives of pelicans, in an interesting way. The birds sat on the gunwales of the open small boats. Each boat had a burning torch on a boom off the bow. The birds dove after fish. The brass collar kept the bird from swallowing their catch, and when it surfaced and jumped back into the boat, the man held a basket forth, touched the bird's head, and it dropped the fish into the basket. Some boats had five to six birds fishing at the same time. They were quite tame and seemed to be well trained. I had read of this ancient Chinese fishing technique in China. It was fascinating to watch.

AMERICA AGAIN

After about twelve days we arrived in the harbor of San Diego, California, on or about 28 February 1946. I had been overseas for two years. Porpoises swam along by the bow of the ship and "guided" us in. Fireboats with all nozzles squirting streams of water came out as a greeting. The *Wakefield* docked, and there was a big sign above the dockside shed that read, "Welcome Home Boys A Job Well Done." It greeted all troopships returning from the Pacific.

There were many civilians, women and girls, on the dock handing cups of milk to each Marine as he came down the gangway. The first milk in two years was delicious. (Milk in China was not cleared by our medical people, so we had to avoid it.)

We boarded small civilian buses for the San Diego Marine Base. I was struck by the healthy, well-dressed appearance of all the civilians we saw. Their bright-colored clothes were in strong contrast to the drab clothing of Chinese civilians.

We passed a line of strikers picketing an aircraft plant along our route. They carried signs complaining about how badly they were treated by the management. It was "like Hitler" one sign read. Not a Marine on the bus murmured a sound, just stared at the strikers. I imagine we were all thinking the same thing— what a bunch of crybabies who did not realize what a soft life they have compared to some people we had seen. In all the years since the war and China Duty, I've never gotten accustomed to civilians complaining about trivial inconveniences.

At the Marine base we were told to turn in our 782 gear and given a list to check off. Anything we didn't turn in we were to declare "lost in combat." I decided to keep my combat pack and my kabar knife, both of which I had carried throughout the war. We were issued campaign ribbons and battle stars, depending on our records.

We were comfortably billeted in recruit huts, given liberty, and told if we behaved no one would order us around. The food was good and we began to relax. In a few days we boarded a troop train for Camp Lejeune, North Carolina, and discharge.

Our train crossed a desert area where there were thousands of parked and abandoned U.S. military aircraft. We traveled miles and miles passing planes of every description.

During one stop in South Carolina, I walked along trackside to stretch my legs. A large older man approached me and struck up a conversation. He was a railroad employee and was attracted by the *fourragere* on my left shoulder, which the Fifth and Sixth Marine Regiments were awarded by France after the First World War. He asked me if I was in the Fifth Marines. I told him yes and he shook my hand. He had been in the same regiment all through World War I. He emphasized what a fine unit it was and their heavy casualties during that conflict. I told him both were true of the regiment in World War II. I boarded the train and we waved goodbye.

We arrived at Camp Lejeune, where we were mustered out of the Marine Corps and given our discharge papers.

The train trip south was a nostalgic one for me. I was a proud American, of course, but I was also a terribly homesick Southerner. The passenger car was filled with my buddies from the Fifth Marines, suddenly civilians again, but Southerners all and homeward bound.

HOME AT LAST

As the train neared Mobile, we began crossing the trestles over the many bayous and swamps north of the city that in earlier days had been a favorite haunt of Creek Indians, fur trappers, and outlaws. Darkness was falling, but I could still see the familiar long-leaf pines on the high ground, and the huge cypresses, black gums, and bay trees in the flooded areas. All were hung with beautiful gray festoons of Spanish moss *(tillandsia usnioides)* gently swaying in the breeze. These swamps were like those I had spent so much time in as a boy, squirrel hunting and "biologizing" in warmer weather, evercautious of cottonmouth moccasins.

As darkness fell, I could well imagine the countless pairs of eyes of such swamp denizens as the black bear, gray fox, bobcat, and deer watching the train as it raced across the trestles with its sparks, long huffing and puffing, billowing thick black smoke, and clickety-clack of the wheels on the rails. I had a warm feeling of finally being back in home country after so long, so far away.

A porter came through our car calling, "Next stop Mow-beel! Next stop Mow-beel!" My buddies in the car shouted "That's you, Sledgehammer." A thrill ran through me—I was finally home after my journey to the abyss. It was hard to realize. There were countless times it had looked as though I would never live to see the next moment, much less live to make it home, and now here we were rolling into the L&N Station, "fugitives from chance's strange arithmetic."

After hurried farewells to my buddies, I raced through the car to the conductor by the exit door at the end of the car. I checked out with the NCO in charge and stepped off the car when he gave the word. I raced alongside the train eagerly looking for Father and Mother, but I did not see them. Presently I saw my brother Edward and Martha, his bride of a few months. She was a real beauty—a tall, slim brunette who had been voted a campus beauty queen at the University of Alabama.

We exchanged warm greetings. Edward was still in his dress uniform of a major in the armored force. He sported an impressive array of ribbons—Silver Star, Bronze Star, three Purple Hearts, and five battle stars. He had been through the meat grinder himself in Europe. One of the first things he said to me was, "God! I don't see how you escaped getting wounded in a Marine rifle company!" (This, incidentally, is a question I've subsequently been asked many times by other combat veterans, and I still don't know the answer. My K/3/5 buddies are convinced that I was spared in order to write their story, *With the Old Breed.*)

As we went to Edward's car, I stopped for a last look at my comrades in combat as the train slowly lurched out of the station. The engineer sounded the locomotive's long, mournful whistle, and I felt a tear roll down my cheek as I waved that last goodbye to the bravest, finest friends I would ever know. I was home, thank the Lord, but now my days with the Fifth Marines, with whom I had shared so much, were over. The sacrifices, terror, and grief we had known had forged deep, abiding bonds between us, and I experienced powerful waves of emotion as the past three years of my life rolled off into the night. This was a major crossroads for me—and I suspect for all of us coming home from overseas combat—closing down one world, opening a starkly contrasting new one with all its uncertainties. I wiped my eyes, took a deep breath, and climbed in Edward's car.

We drove out Government Street, with its beautiful live oak trees meeting overhead and the Spanish moss hanging from every branch. Edward drove us home where he and Martha were presently occupying a private wing. Home was a large, one-story Southern cottage built in 1838 by a family from Georgia as a wedding present for their daughter. Hence the place had always been known as Georgia Cottage. It lay just beyond the city limits.

As we drove through downtown Mobile, the streets were crowded with shoppers, and preparations were underway for the annual Mardi Gras celebrations. In 1946, street crime was almost unknown and after-dark window shopping a common pastime.

Reaching home, we slowly drove up the long driveway lined with huge live oaks waving their ever-present Spanish moss. My heart began pounding at the beauty of Home and my incredible good fortune at living through the unbridled slaughter of Peleliu and Okinawa. There was a fairytale-like unreality about it.

When we pulled up in front of the house, I grabbed my small bag and vaulted up the steps to the front door. Mother stood there smiling in welcome and relief. Captain, her little Boston bull terrier, raced up with one look at me and from about five feet away sprang into my outstretched arms. He immediately began greeting me with happy dog sounds. I hugged him and went to Mother. We embraced as mother and nearly lost son. She marveled at how fit and tanned I was—the Pacific sun had bleached my hair the color of straw and tanned my skin a deep, dark bronze, while the months on occupation duty in China had restored my lost weight.

I was profoundly shocked at Mother's appearance. When I left for the war, she was a pretty, brown-haired lady in the prime of her life, with hardly a wrinkle in her lovely face. Now she was graying and looked careworn.

She took me by the hand and said, "Let's go back and see your father—he can't wait to see you." As we walked through the long hallway, I asked Mother if Father was all right. She replied, yes, but that he was recovering from a bad case of influenza. As I walked into his room, Father leaned forward in his reclining chair to embrace me. In his mid-fifties, robust, and physically fit when I left home, he now looked much older, exhausted, and, like Mother, careworn.

With years of worrying amid fearful news of heavy casualties in Edward's unit and in mine, my parents had nearly broken under the strain. Edward had been wounded three times, and I had been reported missing on Peleliu. Father had asked an Alabama congressman to check the casualty lists to see if I was all right after D-Day; through some error, he told Father I was missing, an inexcusable bureaucratic blunder that caused excruciating pain to my parents for weeks. Nor was my postwar duty in China any relief to their concerns because of the constant armed threat to the Marines wielded by the Chinese Communists. But now, finally, Edward and I were both home.

As I looked at my frail father, I thought about all the hunting trips we had shared in the past when he could walk nearly all day—tiring me and the dogs. He was, like Mother, holding back tears of joy as we embraced. "Will you be all right, Father?" I choked. "Sure, old man just had the damned flu. You look wonderful—do you feel all right? Goodness, Mama, look how he's gained weight!"

I sat down and thanked him for sending me his World War I caliber .45 semiautomatic pistol. I told him how much comfort it had been at night in the confines of a muddy foxhole, listening for the Japanese as they crawled through the nearby brush with knives and grenades. He smiled and nodded.

We sat around and I caught up on local news—who was already home from the war and who had used political influence to stay safely in the United States. "Mama and I are proud of you and Edward, Fritz (his nickname for me)." "Thanks, Father," I said, "I was extremely lucky and I know it." Lord, it was good to be back home again!

After chatting awhile with Captain in my lap, I walked around the house just like old times. It was as though time had stood still—it was as beautiful as I remembered it. I walked out onto the big, screened back porch and looked at the soft floor mat by the door where my late, beloved dog Deacon had always waited patiently for me to come out and take him for a walk or run in the woods and fields. I sighed, still missing that faithful dog.

CIVILIAN LIFE

My adjustment to civilian life was not easy. The freedom to come and go as I pleased was a novel experience for a former rifle-company Marine. Things civilians considered necessities seemed luxuries to me. (Fifty years later I still keenly appreciated the simple luxury of dry socks and clean clothes, a roof over my head, and sleeping in a bed with clean sheets.)

Mother's dog, Captain, who did not know what a flea was, often slept in my bed, and I remembered the painful bites of the fleas on Okinawa, spiteful pests that persisted until, as Ernie Pyle once said, the infantryman becomes so muddy the fleas can't stand him anymore. Captain was both smart and obedient, and it was fun to have a dog around again.

Father was nearly recovered from the flu when he called me in one day. "Sit down, Fritz, I want to talk to you." I assumed he wanted to talk about the war, but that was not the subject on his mind. It turned out to be one of the most memorable conversations of my life.

"Fritz," he said, "I know you have been through an awful experience. I know that nobody had it worse than the First

Marine Division—except maybe those on Bataan and others who were imprisoned. I'm tremendously proud of both you and Edward. You did your duty under terrifying conditions, but you survived in one piece—granted, with some terrible memories you'll have to learn to live with. But take my advice. First, never become embittered because many other men had safe, comfortable war assignments, all too often obtained through political influence. That's the way of cowards in this world. Two, never feel sorry for yourself because of what you endured. On the contrary, feel fiercely proud that you served with the finest and fought against the fiercest enemy, and lived to tell the tale. Three, if you ever drink alcohol, do it in moderation. Alcohol can be a wonderful escape from bad memories, but it is addictive, will make you act the fool, and ultimately ruin you."

His advice was doubly valuable because, during World War I, he had treated shell-shock (combat fatigue) patients in the Army Hospital at Plattsburgh, New York, as a lieutenant colonel in the Medical Corps.

To the last remark I replied, "I know, Father, I've seen that happen to good buddies," recalling some of the worst cases in China. He replied: "Yes, and I've treated some of the nicest people who were ruined by the stuff. But I can't cure them; they must have will power."

He gently slapped me on the knee and said, "Now go take the pointers for some exercise, and always remember what I've told you." I thanked him, and I have since lived by every word of his advice—to my own salvation.

By even the most unbiased judge, my father was a brilliant man. He was a true scientist in his thinking, and he was considered one of the finest physicians in the state. Above all, he was a wonderful father (a stern disciplinarian) and a valuable friend.

I owe Father a great deal. My deep and abiding fascination with the facts and beauties of biological science continues to be the source of peace when old war memories trouble me.

Meanwhile, I still had a long period of adjustment to go through simply to get used to being back home, back in America. Civilian life seemed so strange. People rushed around in a hurry about seemingly insignificant things. Few seemed to realize how blessed they were to be free and untouched by the horrors of war. To them, a veteran was a veteran—all were the same, whether one man had survived the deadliest combat or another had pounded a typewriter while in uniform.

As I strolled the streets of Mobile, I was constantly amazed and pleased at the generally healthy appearance of the civilians. Most people appeared in public in neat, colorful clothing. Their collective appearance contrasted sharply with the multitudes of painfully undernourished and drably attired citizens of China I had seen.

When a Mardi Gras crowd surged into the streets bubbling with enthusiasm over the approaching parade, policemen on foot or motorcycle politely signaled them back to the sidewalks. This was another contrast. In Peiping I saw police wade into such crowds swinging their billy clubs left and right. Men, women, and children who could not back up fast enough because of the press of the crowd received harsh blows to the head, face, or chest. This always infuriated any U.S. Marine present—and our protests incurred puzzlement from the police and only numb appreciation from the people. It was unwise to question the authority of Chinese police—the few locals who did would invariably receive a bloody nose in short order. The behavior of Chinese authorities was a trait I could never understand in that unfortunate country.

Most of my civilian clothes no longer fit well, so I took advantage of a government policy that authorized returning vets to wear their uniforms for their first month in civilian life.

We all wore the "ruptured duck," a cloth insignia of an American eagle with outstretched wings that signified the wearer had been officially discharged from the armed forces. Some army veterans I knew discarded their uniforms as soon as possible. I couldn't blame them. It seemed to me the army could have designed a better outfit for their enlisted troops. Their olive-drab uniform was colorless and usually ill fitting. Even men who tried to sharpen it up had little luck. As for me, I usually wore my dress greens as I had in China. The Marines' dress greens were made of high-quality forest green wool with dark bronze buttons, and they always fit the wearer like a glove—they had to, otherwise the Marine would never be allowed out on liberty. On some occasions I wore my dress blues. This was truly a handsome uniform, and like the dress greens, every aspect reflected a special history or tradition.

Finally, I put away my Marine uniforms and began to acquire a civilian wardrobe. I had to admit that "civvies" were much more comfortable. I especially longed for a clean white shirt. These had not been manufactured during the war economy and were still in short supply a half year after V-J Day.

Among the many veterans in my acquaintances, I observed that the complaining and whining about the hardships of war and military service seemed to be in direct proportion to the distance from life-threatening duty a man had served. I soon realized what Father meant about not becoming embittered. It was difficult to sit with a group of friends and hear some "Stateside commando" complain bitterly about how his corporal had made him carry out the garbage.

Conversation could be risky, I soon found, when some "wannabe" combatant told his tall tales, and I asked him how he felt the first time he saw a buddy killed by a shell. Blank looks from the wannabe and gasps from the girls told me that civilian conversation carried its own perils.

I realized close combat had changed those of us who endured it—we were just plain different from other people through no fault of our own. We saw life through a different lens and always would.

I went to many parties with old high school friends. It was uncanny how the prewar athletic heroes lost their swagger and egotism the moment they clapped eyes on campaign ribbons and battle stars—and the well-known blue diamond with the red numeral one of the First Marine Division patch.

Several of us who had fought as infantry had been too small for football in high school and, though never overtly insulted, had been made aware by heroes of the athletic ilk that we were insignificant and might grow old but never reach a state of manhood. But now, after the supreme test, those of us who had "kept our rendezvous with death" and survived were looked on as men who knew some mystery or secret of life unknown to those whose battles had been limited solely to the athletic field. This was an unforeseen reward for having survived the meat grinder. It added to the warm feeling of being home.

Most civilians in Mobile seemed caught up in the full swing of Mardi Gras. The parades were pretty, but I never got into the spirit of things as I had when I was a child.

February 1946 was cold and damp in Mobile. One very nice party I attended found us seated around the fire while the hostess served delicious hors d'oeuvres such as boiled shrimp and dip—the likes of which many of us had not tasted in years. I was seated next to an attractive couple a little older than I discussing the latest Mardi Gras parade when I noticed the husband kept complaining of his "bad" shoulder. We were all in civilian clothes. I thought the poor guy had been hit in the shoulder and the damp weather was causing him pain. "Were you wounded in the shoulder?" I asked sympathetically. No, he explained, he had been a civilian flight instructor at Maxwell Field in Montgomery, Ala., during the war, and the strict CO of his base had insisted all civilian instructors go on a twenty-mile hike and sleep in pup tents. It seemed there was a cold rain that night, and his shoulder got wet and had been painful ever since. I said with as much sincerity as I could fake: "It is remarkable how well you look after what you've been through. I doubt if most people will ever know the hardships and sacrifices men like you have made for our country." They both thanked me sincerely, but I excused myself, made my thanks to the hostess, and left, not particularly happy with my sense of outrage. I have no doubt our heroic camper is drawing a government pension.

In truth, I missed my old friends from the other world (the "real" world?)—my buddies from the Fifth Marines and especially my "adopted" Soong Taifoo family in Peiping. I recalled that duty fondly. While frequently dangerous, the assignment had proven to be downright pleasant. Occupation duty for me had been almost normal, especially when contrasted to the unholy slaughter pens of Peleliu and Okinawa. But then *nothing* was normal in the daily politico-military struggle for China in those convulsive days.

After my return home in February 1946, I corresponded with my Chinese friends for almost a year. Father Marcel came to the United States and was with Catholic University in Washington, D.C. But Peiping was captured during the victory of the Communists over the Nationalists, and neither Father Marcel nor I ever heard from the Soong family again. I can only fear the worst of fates befell them, and it grieves me deeply that such cultured, educated people fell in the path of the Communist juggernaut.

Father Marcel von Hemelryjck and I corresponded for years,

and he visited my home for several days in 1947. It was wonderful to be with my old friend again, and he was a delight to my parents.

In the late 1940s my letters to Father Marcel were no longer answered. I checked with Catholic University, and a letter followed from a dean telling me Father Marcel had quietly passed away after a short illness. So, as in the war, I lost another fine friend. I can never forget his warm smile, rosy cheeks, and iron handshake. His death saddened me greatly.

The "Real War"

As my life settled down somewhat, I began to think of my future. Rather hastily I decided to go to Auburn (then called Alabama Polytechnic Institute) and major in business. I'll never forget my first day at Auburn.

I was in the Registrar's Office in Sanford Hall. The big room was crowded with long lines of entering students, standing in front of tables, behind which clerks were noting each student's college credits from service schools, determining which might transfer to Auburn.

There was a loud hubbub of voices with about a hundred people in the room. Some men, mostly air corps veterans, had been to various technical schools, and Auburn gave them two years' credit. All veterans were excused from ROTC and physical education.

When I stepped up to the table at the head of the line, a pretty brunette about my age (probably a student's wife) asked pleasantly what schools I had attended in the Marine Corps. I recited all the weapons and tactics schools we had in training. She became more and more disconcerted as she looked in vain on her checklist for anything remotely resembling what I was saying. Finally, in desperation, she slammed her pencil on the table and said in a loud, exasperated voice, "Didn't the Marine Corps teach you anything?!" A gasp ran through the crowd, and you could have heard a pin drop. I didn't lose my temper, but I realized that, like most civilians, war to this lady meant John Wayne or the sweet musical *South Pacific*.

Slowly placing my hands on the table, aware that all eyes were upon us, I said in a loud, calm voice: "Lady, there was a *killing* war. The Marine Corps taught me how to kill Japs and try to survive. Now, if that don't fit into any academic course, I'm sorry. But some of us had to do the killing—and most of my buddies got killed or wounded."

She was speechless. There were many red faces among the obvious noncombatants present. I doubt if there were a half dozen infantrymen or tankers present.

She recovered her composure, looked me in the eye, and said, "I'm so sorry; I apologize; I didn't understand." I told her she was very kind and I did not mean to upset her. "You didn't," she said, "You made me think." So I got credit for ROTC and PE, and the room returned to normal.

The young lady sincerely wished me a long and happy life. I thanked her and left. I felt like some sort of alien, and I realized that this sort of thing would confront me the rest of my days. The war had been so momentous to me, I couldn't imagine anyone not sharing that view—or appreciating the hell I had suffered. In fact, I was totally unprepared for how rapidly most Americans who did not experience combat would forget about the war, the evils we faced, and how incredibly tough it had been for us to defeat the Japanese and the Nazis. I didn't realize how swiftly most Americans would once again take their freedom for granted.

Developing a Postwar Life

Like many other veterans, I made a false start in college. I earned a business degree from Auburn, still unaware that in my heart of hearts, I was a "born biologist." I worked hard, graduated in three years, then returned to Mobile to labor in the insurance office of a long-suffering family friend, who tried valiantly to teach me the ropes. Neither of us knew that I was an embryonic naturalist and by no means a businessman, so we both tried to make a go of this for two years despite a disappointing record of progress.

One evening Father sat me down for a friendly appraisal. With his deep knowledge of human nature, he suggested, "Fritz, why don't you write Auburn and inquire about entering one of their graduate biological programs? But don't become a medical doctor! The damned government is going to keep messing with it until they bring about socialized medicine and drive both physicians and patients to distraction." His words illuminated a new path for me—I was intrigued with the possibility of becoming a biological scientist.

In short order, the shift in directions opened wondrous new doors. I met the girl of my dreams during someone else's wedding, of all things. My good friend Nick Holmes was getting married in Mobile and asked me to be his best man. I gladly agreed. I was even more glad when I met one of the bridesmaids, Miss Jeanne Arceneaux. We were so smitten with each other from the start that we could barely concentrate on our responsibilities at Nick's wedding. In fact, another wedding—ours—followed shortly. We were married on 12 March 1952, and it was the happiest, smartest move I ever made.

We moved to Auburn while I worked on earning my master's degree, and then we moved on to the University of Florida for my Ph.D. in zoology with a minor in biochemistry. The arrival of our two sons, John Sturdivant and William Henry, made our lives complete. In 1962 I joined the faculty of the University of Montevallo, and we settled down in the quiet little college town in the foothills of central Alabama. There we have enjoyed a full and joyous life together.

Jeanne shared my dreams—and endured my many years of vivid nightmares. She helped me fulfill the destiny that I inherited twice—once at birth, again by surviving Peleliu and Okinawa. Life with Jeanne, mastering the mysteries of biology, and teaching thousands of gifted young students have all been as drastically far removed from Bloody Nose Ridge and Kunishi Ridge as Heaven is from Hell.

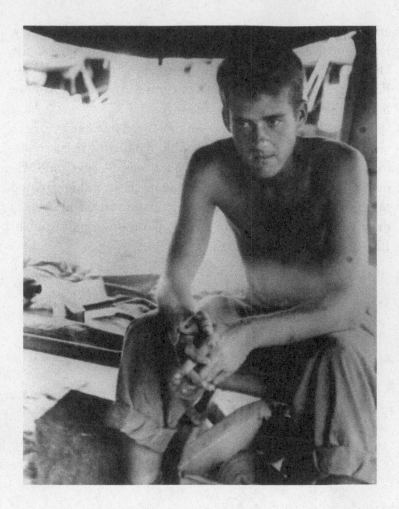

Author at the end of the eighty-two-day Okinawa campaign "trying to comprehend a world without war." Occupation duty in China came next. June 1945. *Courtesy Jeanne Sledge.*

A U.S. Marine hoists a child as admiring civilians and police look on. The policeman on the right carries a German Mauser automatic pistol in his long wooden holster. Tientsin, October 1945. *Courtesy U.S. Marine Corps.*

The main gate at Engua Fu, the English Legation, where the
Marines of the 3/5 were billeted. Complete with a wall as pro-
tection from bandits, the place was "haunted by the spirit of
Rudyard Kipling." *Courtesy Jeanne Sledge.*

Author and Hao Ching Fu, the company's houseboy, at the
English Legation in Peiping. The two became fast friends and
taught each other their respective languages. 1945.
Courtesy Jeanne Sledge.

Observing that "the average farm mule in Alabama had a far easier life than a Chinese rickshaw coolie," author gives a driver a break. Peiping, November 1945. *Courtesy Jeanne Sledge.*

Author on guard duty with his "World War II constant companion," a Thompson submachine gun. Lang Fang, 1945.
Courtesy Jeanne Sledge.

A 1945 view of the main gate to Peiping's Forbidden City, "a fabled castle in a storybook." *Courtesy Jeanne Sledge.*

There was "little evidence of vandalism" in the Forbidden City since the Japanese feared provoking riots, but they did scrape the gold plating from these massive bronze fishbowls. Peiping, 1945. *Courtesy Jeanne Sledge.*

Peiping was full of architectural wonders such as this gate a Marine truck passes through. 1945. *Courtesy Jeanne Sledge.*

Lantienchang Airfield, author bundled up against the cold while "protecting air corps glamour boys." Peiping, January 1946. *Courtesy Jeanne Sledge.*

Left to right: Anna Soong, Margaret Soong, Dr. Y. K. Soong, Father Marcel von Hemelryjck. These extraordinary people provided the "warmest setting and friendship" as well as a bridge back to civilization after months of killing.

Peiping, winter 1946. Courtesy Jeanne Sledge.

EPILOGUE

I Am Not the Man I Would Have Been

Looking back over those momentous events of fifty years ago when I was a Marine evokes strong emotions. The years immediately after the war were the hardest. As Paul Fussell remarked, the combat veteran not only has to survive the experience, he has to learn to live with it the rest of his life. He was so right. For the first twenty-odd years after my return, nightmares occurred frequently, waking me either crying or yelling, always sweating, and with a pounding heart. Some nights I delayed going to bed, dreading the inevitable nightmares. Old comrades wrote me that similar troubles drove many of them to drink and to the ensuing misery of alcoholism, which they beat with sheer self-discipline.

Science was my salvation! During many of those years, I was a graduate student in biology—first earning my M.S. degree at Auburn, then my Ph.D. at the University of Florida. It was like an intellectual boot camp; standards were high. I found quite by accident that after a day of concentrating intensely on some difficult problem in biology or biochemistry, the war nightmares did not come that night. I also found that a conversation about the war with a veteran was a likely cause for night-mares—unless I applied my mind to some fact of biology or biochemistry before bedtime. An hour's intense concentration on science resulted in a peaceful night's sleep. Often I would listen to records of some of the intricate keyboard music of J. S. Bach or the orchestral works of W. A. Mozart, and my mind was put completely at peace. Eventually, I managed to conquer the curse of combat nightmares.

In later years some memory of the war has flashed through my mind nearly every day. Old buddies tell me it has been the same with them. However, if my thoughts become too worri-some, I apply the above formula, which acts like oil on troubled waters even though nightmares rarely visit me anymore. But if one does not watch himself, depression can become a problem too. Needless to say, I read as little about World War II and watch as little film about it as possible.

The war left me with a deep appreciation for the simple things in life. Putting on a pair of clean, dry socks is one of the greatest luxuries I know. A shave, a warm shower, and sleeping in a sheeted bed are, too. When it is raining, especially on an autumn day, I look out the window at the falling drops and my thoughts sometimes drift back to those awful days on Oki-nawa—Snafu and I bailing out a muddy foxhole with an old helmet, shivering in a torrential cold rain, and both of us cring-ing as each Japanese shell came screaming into the corpse-strewn area to explode with a deafening crash. I quickly bring the focus of my mind back to the present and thank God I do not have to suffer such hardship and misery again. And, oh, what a blessing to be relieved of constant terror!

My love of the outdoors was strangely affected by the war—the way I looked at my surroundings was altered. My view of the outdoors had taken on more of an analytical perspective of its features as military terrain—likely areas for the placement of various foxholes, the company 60mm mortars to cover defilades, the light machine guns so as to achieve crossfires along the company front, fields of fire, and possible avenues of enemy attack or ambush. This change in outlook was intense in the early years home, but I cleared my mind of it by concentrating on plant and animal species present or probable. But the old combat view of things still creeps in sometimes after more than fifty years.

My feelings about one of my prewar hobbies, hunting, were completely changed by my combat experience. Father and I had hunted quail, mourning dove, and squirrels primarily. He had taught me a great deal about the habits of wild game and the outdoors, and I had been thrilled with our trips afield. He was a fine shot with either a rifle or shotgun and taught me well.

After my return home, he and I went on a dove hunt west of Mobile. The field was owned by one of Father's patients, who permitted only Father and his guests to hunt there. This particular trip was my first and last dove hunt after the war, so I remember it vividly.

Although Father owned fine automatic shotguns, .20-, .16-, and .12-gauge, my gun of choice for doves was a single-shot .410. It did not have a long range or as big a shot pattern as the larger gauges, but I either hit the bird or missed it—fewer cripples. Doves fly rapidly and are beautifully streamlined in flight. I had to learn to shoot at a rapidly flying dove so that it was in the middle of the fairly small shot pattern. As the gun held only a single shell, the shot either bagged the bird or he was out of range in a split second. Gunners with larger caliber automatics often banged away at the same bird with all three shells and missed. On hunts consisting of several gunners, I was invariably advised (when a young teenager) to get a bigger shotgun for doves. "You can't hit anything flying fast with that pea shooter." As boys were taught then, "Respect your elders—and no sassy backtalk." I always grinned and said, "Yes, sir."

After dove hunting with Father and taking his advice, my .410 rarely missed. In those days, as I recall, a box of shotgun shells held twenty-five shells, and the game limit on doves was fourteen birds per hunter. I practiced hard, carefully selected my shots, and usually got my limit by firing fifteen shells, with ten shells left over. Father was very proud of my marksman-ship—hitting a fast-flying dove was a difficult shot for anyone.

Many times when the hunt was over at sunset and we unloaded our guns and then put our birds in separate piles before dividing up the game equally, the hunters who had been on a stand near me would stare at my number of birds and say, "Boy, where did you get all them birds (doves)? I hardly heard you shooting more than a dozen times and I shot up 2 boxes of shells to get my limit!" I would grin and say I was just lucky. Father would wink at me and smile with pride. I always com-peted with myself, choosing my targets carefully, firing, and fol-lowing through—trying to get my limit with as few shells as possible. I never just banged away like some hunters.

On the first dove hunt with Father after the war, I put only fifteen shells in my game bag and left the remaining ten in the box in the car. I didn't tell Father, but I wanted to see if my years of rifle shooting in the Marine Corps had spoiled my ability as a wing shot. I knelt beside an old fence overgrown with vines and knee-high broom sage on the edge of the cornfield. Father moved farther along the fence and secreted himself in a similar manner. The sun was just rising; it was a cold bright day. Some doves came flashing over to alight in the field and feed on spilled corn kernels. I was amazed at how streamlined and fast they were. Father was shooting sparingly—he was an even better shot than I was. Every time he shot, I saw a dove fold its wings and pitch to the ground. When I fired at my tenth bird, he folded his wings like all the others and slanted rapidly down, hitting the ground with a thump. I felt my shell compartment and counted five shells. Ten shots and ten kills—I hadn't forgotten my wing shooting technique after all.

I had, as usual, marked where the last dove fell. I went out to pick it up. This bird was still alive—it was lying on its side with its head erect, and I knew he was badly injured because I could see him gasping for air. Slowly I picked up the dove, my hand was wet with blood. I looked at the dove's head. The bright sun shone clearly on the beautiful dark brown eyes bordered by the pale blue fleshy eyelids as the bird gasped for air. "My Lord! You poor thing—and you couldn't even shoot back!" When a dove hunter held an injured bird, the procedure to prevent further suffering was to grip the bird's body and hit its head hard against the gunstock, killing the bird instantly. This I did, bagged the dead bird. I pressed the ejector lever on my gun; the empty shell ejected. Ten shells, ten doves.

I slowly walked out of the field to the old hunting car parked nearby. I laid my gun on the grass and sat on the running board of the old Ford. I fought hard to hold back the tears as they ran down my face—my mind's eye still clearly seeing those beautiful brown eyes bordered by those fleshy pale blue eyelids. Father came hurrying over to my "stand" by the fence and called me. I called to him and he came over to the car. He was concerned as to why I left the field, but when he saw the tears, he said, "What's the matter, Fritz?" I mumbled, "I just can't kill 'em anymore, Pop! I can't bear to see 'em suffer. I'm sorry, but I'm through with hunting!" "You do *not* need to apologize to me or anyone. If that's the way you feel, you've earned the right to do as you please about hunting and it's nobody's business but yours." He suggested we have some hot chocolate, for I was shivering. Finally, he put his hand on my shoulder and said, "How many shells and how many birds?" "Ten and ten," I replied. "Well, well, you always were damn good! Now you're even better. But maybe it's time to quit, you don't have anything else to prove about wing shooting—and it'll relieve the dove population, I'm sure," he laughed. That wonderful, kind doctor who I was so lucky to have as a father knew the war had changed me more than I realized. After all, during World War I, he was considered an expert at treating shell-shock cases from France.

Some time later I discussed my feelings about hunting with Father. The depth of his understanding amazed me. "You've just seen too much suffering, Fritz, why don't you take up bird watching as a hobby—and nobody gets hurt." I took his advice and never shot another dove but banded them for the Conservation Department and fed them in my yard all year round.

I had one other experience as a hunter (my last) shortly after I returned home. A long-time friend and patient of Father's, Mr. Augustine Meaher, invited me on a deer hunt at his hunting preserve known as "The Promised Land." Gus owned several thousand acres of deep forest along the Mobile and Tensaw Rivers (the Tensaw was an Indian tribe that had occupied the area in the sixteenth and seventeenth centuries). His property had been a huge ancestral plantation after settlers removed the Indians west, but no farming had been done there since the Civil War, and the area was covered with trackless forests harboring deer, black bear, and countless game and nongame species. It is a fascinating area and a biologist's paradise.

Gus had a successful business in Mobile and used the area primarily for deer hunting—sometimes inviting ten to twelve guests. I had no desire to shoot a deer, but Father asked me to go because Gus extended the invitation to both of us; Father had a spell of flu and could not make the trip, so I accepted the invitation. Actually, it was considered quite a privilege to be invited on one of these trips because they were fabulous affairs—like a sporting event in the nineteenth century—with at least a dozen servants and a fine pack of deer hounds, numbering about fifteen to twenty dogs. Every living thing—servants, hounds, and guests—was a certifiable character, with a nickname that always seemed to fit the individual. This was primarily because Gus had a wonderful sense of humor. Throughout the entire day, he carried on an endless, witty banter with the servants, guests, and even the hounds. In addition, he was one of the most well-read people I ever knew. It was fascinating to hear him discuss the history of The Promised Land, what was known about the local Indians and their trading customs in the earlier years.

Gus picked me up before daylight and we drove to Mount Vernon, a little town north of Mobile. Then it was off through woodland roads to the riverbank, where we loaded our gear in several boats for the crossing to the hunting camp. Frost covered everything in the pale light of dawn. The head boatman, Jim (who was a Negro preacher, burial-insurance agent, and one-time deputy sheriff as well as Gus's foreman around the property), squared everybody away in the boats and saw to the life preservers. At this point the river was about one hundred yards wide and sometimes rather choppy.

We crossed the river and unloaded. Gus rode in a World War II jeep and drove each of us to his stand. Each hunter got out of the jeep, and Gus instructed him where to expect a deer running in front of the drive (hounds followed by their handlers). Gus was no-nonsense when he told each hunter not to leave his stand until called for and to remain still and quiet once the hounds began baying and the drivers began shouting "Whoop, whoop" to start the deer. (A hunter wandering around the woods could be shot by an inexperienced person who fired at any movement instead of at a certain, clear target. This sort of thing had never happened on Gus's place, and he made as certain as he could that it never did.)

After everyone was on his stand (which reminded me of sentry duty), the drive began. The drivers shouted and whooped, and when the hounds picked up a deer trail, they began baying. The baying of a hound is a wonderful sound. It bears no resemblance to a hound barking but is a sustained, deep-throated "whoop, baroop, ooop," and each hound's voice can be recognized by the owner or drivers. When a dog struck a hot trail, its voice became excited and the syllables closer together. When a hound found an older trail, he usually announced it with a periodic "baroop," then silence for possibly several minutes, then "baroop," and so on.

What was music to me was terror to the harried deer, which ran and bounded away as fast as it could run. I heard the hounds to my front getting excited as they approached. One sounded "baroop, baroop." Then I heard the deer bounding through the underbrush. It sounded like several men crashing through the area. I peeped around the tree I was standing by and saw a medium-sized deer with spike antlers bounding toward me with what looked to be twenty-foot leaps. As the buck entered a small clearing, I stepped out and aimed just in front of the heart area. The buck saw me and rolled his big terrified eyes so that I could see the whites. Just as I began squeezing the trigger, he jumped into the next bounding motion. I aimed, led the deer with the front sight, squeezed off the shot, and "followed through" as he was in the air. The shotgun roared and the buck was dead before he crashed into a thicket at the edge of the clearing.

I looked at that beautiful, graceful animal driven into my ambush by the hounds and thought, "Is this sport?" I felt like I had shot a cow in a pasture. Several hounds ran up to the deer, sniffed it, and then milled around, totally uninterested in the dead deer. They had been bred to trail the game, not eat or attack it. Someone yelled, "Did you shoot a deer, Gene?" I answered yes, and within a few minutes several drivers and other hunters were milling around and commenting on the probable age and weight of the buck. The hounds milled around, wagging their tails and panting. Several men congratulated me—and I was the least excited of them all. If I had made the shot with a rifle, it would have required skill—but to lie in wait as a terrified deer ran for his life right into an ambush, where it was unlikely he could escape a spread of buckshot rather than one rifle bullet, hardly seemed like sport.

At lunch I told Gus deer hunting with a shotgun was not for me. So he said for the afternoon hunt he would have Jim take me by boat to a spot where thick woods came down to the riverbank and deer frequently swam across. I could take my rifle because the deer drive that afternoon would be in another area and drivers and hounds would not be in any danger of my firing.

Jim took me in the large skiff downriver about a mile and turned into a small growth of cane where the water was shallow. He wished me luck and told me what time he would pick me up. I took up my stand in a patch of cane with the river to my back and a small pond to my front at the forest's edge. The trees were large and visibility was good for quite a distance. Soon I heard the afternoon drive begin, the hounds far away to my right. My area was quiet except for a beautiful pair of wood ducks playing and searching for food in the pond. An occasional squirrel ran down one tree and up another. Suddenly, I heard loud sloshing like several people were walking in shallow water. Two beautiful does appeared, walking briskly through the water as they exited the woods and stopped at the far edge of the pond about thirty yards away. They kept looking toward the area of the drive and moving their ears to capture every sound possible. More loud sloshing of water, and two does and a large buck came up to the first does and stopped. They finally looked in my direction. I remained still, and since the wind was blowing toward me, the deer could not pick up my scent. They stood motionless, staring at me and standing in the clump of cane. They seemed more concerned with the baying of the hounds than with me, though.

Because of the way I held my rifle, I could see my wristwatch, so I timed the action, or inaction, of the deer. One of the does picked up an acorn at the edge of the pond and ate it. The buck was large and had a fine set of antlers, the eight points gleaming in the light. Slowly I raised my rifle and sighted in on his chest—no, he was too fine a creature to kill. I had murdered one of his kind that morning, so I did not need the venison. Slowly, I lowered my rifle. The buck remained motionless—his instincts probably told him no shape such as he saw in the cane was natural. Deer, like most mammals, have very poor sight, except for detecting motion, and are primarily colorblind.

For fifteen minutes we stared at each other. A shot in the air would send them springing away into the woods. But a shot would frighten them, which I had no desire to do. The deer seemed more curious than afraid. They kept sniffing the air, which apparently bore no scent of danger. I had on waterproof boots but was beginning to get cold. Finally, I needed to move a little. I knew that as soon as I did, they would bolt. So I whistled softly. Every big ear quickly turned in my direction. I whistled softly again. All the deer slowly lowered their ears, turned, went sloshing onto higher ground, and ambled into the woods, looking back at me once or twice. The whole episode is one of my most cherished memories.

When Jim picked me up in the boat, he asked if I had seen a deer. I said no, not wanting to tell him I had seen five. When we returned to camp, several people asked what I had seen, and I reported a few squirrels and some wood ducks. If I had told those eager hunters what really had happened, they would have elected to throw me into the river.

Gus didn't allow any drinking during hunting hours. So after the guns were all unloaded and put into their cases, the bottled spirits were brought forth and the partiers had a ball; each of the weary hounds went to the fenced yard, jumped up on the raised platforms, and went into his barrel for a nap. The platform was raised as protection against high water as well as alligators—which have a special appetite for dog flesh.

We recrossed the river after much conviviality and scattered to our homes. So ended my last deer hunt, with the memory of that beautiful buck and his harem down the river. I have wondered how long he survived.

I am not antihunting as long as it is managed by wildlife experts. Most game animals outproduce their food supply, and since civilization has destroyed most of the natural predators, starvation results unless populations are controlled by game management overseeing proper hunting practices. But the terrified eyes of that spike buck I shot are something I'd like to forget. I have felt the same terror when being shot at—so hunting is not for me.

World War II gave me a convenient measuring stick for duty, courage, terror, friendship, patience, horror, endurance, compassion, discomfort, grief, and pain that has remained with me daily. The English poet Robert Graves said World War I affected him in much the same way. Anyone who has not suffered the prolonged fear and limitless fatigue that was the combat infantryman's lot might find this difficult to comprehend.

Over fifty years later I look back on the war as though it

were some giant killing machine into which we were thrown to endure fear to the brink of insanity—some fell over the brink—and physical fatigue to near collapse. Those who survived unhurt will never forget—and cannot forget—the many friends lost in their prime and the many articles of civilization ruthlessly destroyed.

As I look back, some facts are quite clear: Japan's sneak bombing of Pearl Harbor destroyed many American lives, ships, and planes. We had no choice but to destroy Imperial Japan. The A-bomb ended that war. It saved millions of American lives by preventing a murderous invasion of Japan and the probable destruction of a suicidal Japanese population. The Japanese soldier was a bloodthirsty foe imbued with the Code of Bushido (Code of the Warrior) and *yamata damashii* (the fighting power of Japan). If we had not defeated an army that thought it was unbeatable, who knows how many American cities might have shared the horrid Rape of Nanking. (Skeptical revisionists may laugh if they wish.)

In looking back, I am still amazed I escaped the killing machine. Why I never fell killed or wounded in that storm of steel thrown at us countless times still astonishes me. I am proud of the number of the enemy I fired on and hit with my mortar, rifle, or Tommy gun—and regret the ones I missed. There is no "mellowing" for me—that would be to forgive all the atrocities the Japanese committed against millions of Asians and thousands of Americans. To "mellow" is to forget.

Each man who survived, I am certain, was plucked from the mire of death by the Almighty—and in this I feel humble and grateful.

Socrates said, "Know Thyself." I do. The war taught me.
Finis.

FOR FURTHER READING

Alexander, Joseph H. *Storm Landings: Epic Amphibious Battles in the Central Pacific.* Annapolis: Naval Institute Press, 1997.

Alexander, Joseph H., with Don Horan and Norman C. Stahl. *A Fellowship of Valor: The Battle History of the United States Marines.* New York: HarperCollins, 1997.

Daws, Gavin. *Prisoners of the Japanese: POWs of World War II in the Pacific.* New York: William Morrow, 1995.

Denson, John V., ed. *The Costs of War: America's Pyrrhic Victories.* New Brunswick, N.J.: Transaction, 1997.

Feifer, George. *Tennozan: The Battle of Okinawa and the Atomic Bomb.* New York: Ticknor and Fields, 1992.

Frank, Benis M., and Henry I. Shaw Jr. *Western Pacific Operations.* Vol. 5 of *History of U.S. Marine Corps Operations in World War II.* Washington: HQMC, 1968.

Hallas, James H. *The Devil's Anvil: The Assault on Peleliu.* Westport, Conn.: Praeger, 1994.

Harris, Merion, and Suzie Harris. *Soldiers of the Sun: The Rise and Fall of the Imperial Japanese Army.* New York: Random House, 1991.

Jones, Wilbur D., Jr. *Gyrene: The World War II United States Marine.* Shippensburg, Pa.: White Mane, 1998.

Linderman, Gerald F. *The World Within War: America's Combat Experience in World War II*. New York: Free Press, 1997.

McMillan, George. *The Old Breed: A History of the First Marine Division in World War II*. Washington: Infantry Journal Press, 1949.

Shaw, Henry I., Jr. *The United States Marines in North China, 1945–49*. Washington: HQMC, 1968.

Simmons, Edwin H. *The United States Marines: A History*. 3d ed. Annapolis: Naval Institute Press, 1998.

Sledge, E. B. *With the Old Breed at Peleliu and Okinawa*. Classics of Naval Literature. 1981. Reprint, Annapolis: Naval Institute Press, 1996.

INDEX

Numbers in italics refer to illustrations.